The Toll-houses
of Cambridgeshire

Patrick Taylor

POLYSTAR PRESS

ISBN 978 1 907154 06 5

The Toll-houses of Cambridgeshire

Published by
Polystar Press
277 Cavendish Street
Ipswich Suffolk IP3 8BQ
(01473) 434604
polystar@ntlworld.com

ISBN 978 1 907154 06 5

All rights reserved.
This book is protected by copyright.
No part of it may be reproduced, stored in a
retrieval system, or transmitted, in any form
or by any means, electronic, mechanical,
photocopying, recording or otherwise, without
the written permission of the author or publisher.

Every attempt has been made to trace accurate
ownership of copyrighted material in this book.
Errors and omissions will be corrected in
subsequent editions, provided that
notification is sent to the publisher.

© Patrick Taylor 2011

Typeset by nattygrafix

Printed by
R Booth
The Praze, Penryn

Contents

Illustrations

section

			page
0.0	Introduction	TrumpingtonToll-house, Cambridge	1
1.0	**The Turnpike Roads**	Mending the Highways	2
		Statute for Mending of Highways, 1555	3
1.1	The King's Highway	Salisbury Coach Service Poster	4
1.2	Parish Responsibility	New Bridges, St Ives	5
1.3	Available Technology	London Wheel Act, 1690	6
1.4	Justice Trusts	Wansford Bridge, River Nene	7
1.5	Turnpike Trusts	First Turnpike Act, 1663	8
1.6	Turnpike Mania	Turnpike Boundary Stone, Ely	9
		Toll-house Sale Poster, 1872	10
1.7	Winding Up	Toll-house Sale Poster, 1871	11
2.0	**Collecting The Tolls**	Toll Gate Collection	12
		Toll Board from Sussex	13
2.1	Toll Gates & Turnpikes	Toll Farming Poster, 1862	14
2.2	Toll-houses	Porch Window, Wintringham	15
		Varieties of Toll Gate	16
2.3	Local Distinctiveness	Limestone Toll-house, Plymouth	17
2.4	What Lies Ahead?	Varieties of Roof Pitch and Materials	19
3.0	**The Cambs Turnpikes**	Stagecoach and Four	20
		Toll Board, Stretham	21
3.1	Cambs Turnpike Trusts	Milestone, Peterborough	22
		Godmanchester Turnpike Stone	23
3.2	Limestone and Clay	The Geology of Cambridgeshire	24,25
3.3	Timber, Brick and Tile		26
3.4	Cambs Toll-houses	Carstone, White Brick and Slate	27
4.0	**A Cambs Gazetteer**	Memorial, Burwell Ness Toll Gate	28
		The Turnpike Roads of Cambs	29,30
		Cambridge - Ely etc.	31-37
		Chatteris Ferry - Somersham etc.	38,39
		Chatteris Ferry - Wisbech etc.	40-44
		Wisbech - South Lynn	45
		Wisbech - Thorney	46
		Peterborough - Thorney	48
		Royston - Wansford Bridge	48-57
		Peterborough - Oundle	49
		Market Harborough - Brampton etc.	50,51
		Bury - Stratton	53-56
		Great Staughton - Wellingborough	58
		Potton - St Neots - Cambridge	59,60
		Cambridge - Arrington Bridge - Potton	60,61
		Chesterford - Newmarket / Cambridge	63-65
		Godmanchester - Newmarket Heath	65,66
		Haverhill - Shelford	66,67
5.0	Appendix: The Impostors		69
6.0	Bibliography		79

for all who sailed on
STS Malcolm Miller

0.0 Introduction

As long ago as 1978, when I was fresh out of architectural school and living in Cornwall, it was resolved that toll-houses would be a worthwhile subject for further study - "one day" was the term used at the time I believe. Years passed, life was got on with, and it was not until 1992 when living in Suffolk, that I went to study for an MA in Conservation Studies at York University.

Here I encountered the phenomenon of local distinctiveness and realised that the toll-houses, built for the most part during the early industrial revolution before the coming of the railways, might be a good indicator. My dissertation in 1995 followed this hunch through and included as part of my study of local distinctiveness, a comparison between the toll-houses in the two counties I knew best, Cornwall and Suffolk.

My first two books on toll-houses, covering Cornwall and Suffolk in turn, drew heavily on that dissertation, consisting mainly of extracts relevant to each county, together with new gazetteer sections based on my research for the dissertation. For this Cambridgeshire volume along similar lines, my thanks must go to Milestone Society members Grainne Farrington (Cambs), Mike Hallett (newsletter), Michael Knight (Beds) and Alan Rosevear (database). Also very helpful were Bill Wakefield and Keith Hinde (Stretham Engine Trust), Bridget Flanagan (local historian), Gordon Richardson (toll-house owner) and the respective staffs of the Cambridge and Huntingdon Record Offices.

Having recently completed further toll-house books on Norfolk and Essex, Cambridgeshire with its borders shared with both those counties and Suffolk seemed the next place within reach it would be sensible to look at. Beyond here, unless I move, any further books will have to be collaborations, as has been done successfully for Devon and is ongoing currently for Somerset. One day maybe we will join up across the country, east meeting west, but there is a lot of ground to cover yet.

Gault brick Toll-house,
Trumpington, Cambridge
photo: polystar

1

1.0 The Turnpike Roads

Mending the Highways
(from Smith - 1970)

CAP. VIII.
The ftatute for mending of highways.

FOR amending of highways, being now both very noifom and tedious to travel in, and dangerous to all paffengers and carriages :

(2) Be it enacted by the authority of this prefent parliament, that the conftables and church-wardens of every parifh within this realm, fhall yearly upon the *Tuefday* or *Wednefday* in *Eafter* week call together a number of the parifhioners, and fhall then elect and chufe two honeft perfons of the parifh to be furveyors and orderers for one year, or the works for amendment of the highways in their parifh leading to any market-town ; (3) the which perfons fhall have authority by virtue hereof, to order and direct the perfons and carriages that fhall be appointed for thofe works, by their difcretions ; (4) and the faid perfons fo named fhall take upon them the execution of their faid offices, upon pain every of them making default, to forfeit twenty fhillings.

Who fhall be charged towards the mending of highways. Surveyors fhall be appointed for the amendment of highways. 3 Mod. 96. 22Car.2.c.12. f. 12.

II. And the faid conftables and church-wardens fhall then alfo name and appoint four days for the amending of the faid ways, before the feaft of the nativity of Saint *John Baptift* then next following; (2) and fhall openly in the church the next *Sunday* after *Eafter* give knowledge of the fame four days ; (3) and upon the faid days the parifhioners fhall endeavour themfelves to the amending of the faid ways ; (4) and fhall be chargeable thereunto as followeth ; that is to fay, every perfon for every plow-land in tillage or pafture that he or fhe fhall occupy in the fame parifh, and every other perfon keeping there a draught or plough, fhall find and fend at every day and place to be appointed for the amending of the ways in that parifh as is aforefaid, one wain or cart furnifhed after the cuftom of the country with oxen, horfes or other cattle, and all other neceffaries meet to carry things convenient for that purpofe, and alfo two able men with the fame, upon pain of every draught making default, ten fhillings; (5) and every other houfholder, and alfo every cottager and labourer of that parifh, able to labour, and being no hired fervant by the year, fhall by themfelves or one fufficient labourer for every of them, upon every of the faid four days, work and travel in the amendment of the faid highways, upon pain of every perfon making default, to lofe for every day twelve pence. (6) And if the faid carriages of the parifh, or any of them, fhall not be thought needful by the fupervifors to be occupied upon any of the faid days, that then every fuch perfon that fhould have fent any fuch carriage, fhall fend to the faid work for every carriage fo fpared two able men, there to labour for that day, upon pain to lofe for every man fo fent to the faid work, twelve pence. (7) And every perfon and carriage abovefaid fhall have and bring with them fuch fhovels, fpades, picks, mattocks,

Four days fhall be appointed for the amendment of highways. Six days are appointed by 5El.c.13.f.7. Each perfon's charge towards the mending of highways. Explained by 18 El. c. 10; f. 2.

Neceffary tools fhall be brought to be

Statute for Mending of Highways, 1555
(from Serjeant & Penrose - 1973)

1.1 The King's Highway

In order to understand the turnpike road system that gave rise to toll-houses in the eighteenth century we need first to look at its origins in the mists of medieval time.

Early roads were not actual parcels of real estate set aside for the purpose of transit as have evolved today, but rather lines of least resistance where a 'right of passage' existed - the King's Highway - over ground that remained in private ownership. This still exists in vestigial form in our modern footpath network, which then as now consisted of three levels of usage: footpaths, bridleways and carriageways (now roads used as public paths). In those days diversions were implemented to maintain the right of the traveller if the road was 'founderous' or his way was blocked, rather than at the request of the owner to suit the management of the land as is now often the case.

The highway was thus a 'communal property right' available freely for the use of any subject of the Crown and as such received little or no maintenance other than out of selfish necessity to overcome a particular obstacle such as a flood or fallen tree. It was therefore in no individual's interest to invest time or money in repairing something that would mainly benefit others.

As a consequence the roads were generally in a very poor state and greatly abused by heavy loads with many horses, by spiked or narrow wheels and by the dragging of sledges or timber. Similar problems exist to this day where the selfish interest of highway users will require legislation to achieve a benefit for the common good (e.g. the limitation of motor car use), and it was indeed legislation then that was a first step on the way to improvement of the situation. A parallel can be seen here with another communal property right, that of the old strip field system with attendant grazing and hunting rights, which was also abused by selfish interest and eventually put to rights by the legislation of the Enclosure Acts.

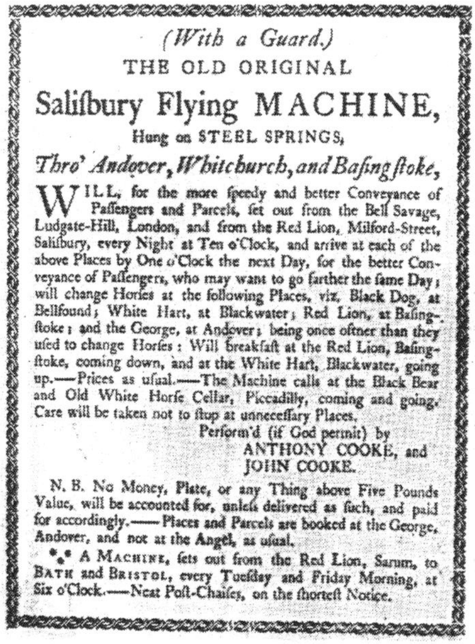

(With a Guard.)
THE OLD ORIGINAL
Salisbury Flying MACHINE,
Hung on STEEL SPRINGS,
Thro' Andover, Whitchurch, and Basing stoke,
WILL, for the more speedy and better Conveyance of Passengers and Parcels, set out from the Bell Savage, Ludgate-Hill, London, and from the Red Lion, Milford-Street, Salisbury, every Night at Ten o'Clock, and arrive at each of the above Places by One o'Clock the next Day, for the better Conveyance of Passengers, who may want to go farther the same Day; will change Horses at the following Places, viz. Black Dog, at Bellfound; White Hart, at Blackwater; Red Lion, at Basing-stoke; and the George, at Andover; being once oftner than they used to change Horses: Will breakfast at the Red Lion, Basing-stoke, coming down, and at the White Hart, Blackwater, going up.——Prices as usual.——The Machine calls at the Black Bear and Old White Horse Cellar, Piccadilly, coming and going. Care will be taken not to stop at unnecessary Places.
Perform'd (if God permit) by
ANTHONY COOKE, and
JOHN COOKE.
N. B. No Money, Plate, or any Thing above Five Pounds Value, will be accounted for, unless delivered as such, and paid for accordingly.——Places and Parcels are booked at the George, Andover, and not at the Angel, as usual.
⁎ A MACHINE, sets out from the Red Lion, Sarum, to BATH and BRISTOL, every Tuesday and Friday Morning, at Six o'Clock.——Neat Post-Chaises, on the shortest Notice.

Salisbury Coach Service Poster
(from Wright - 1992)

1.2 Parish Responsibility

In the mid sixteenth century the state of the roads became of such concern that legislation was passed to firmly place the responsibility for their repair in the hands of the parish in which they were situated. The initial Act of 1555, in the brief reign of Mary Tudor, was a temporary measure which required each parish to elect two Surveyors. Their duty was to oversee the repair of roads by the inhabitants of that parish on four days per year when they were to provide 'statute labour'.

The larger landowners were also required to provide two men plus carts and tools whilst the Surveyors were permitted to dig for gravel on any waste land or commons adjoining the road. A further Act of 1562 extended the statute duties to six days per year and defaulters were liable to heavy fines.

Parishes that failed to maintain their roads properly were liable to be presented by the Justices to Quarter Sessions. If they then still failed to repair the roads satisfactorily they would be subject to indictment and the imposition of fines and/or additional days of statute labour. An occasional alternative to this was the raising of a Highway Rate by the Justices, which would then be used to pay for the necessary labour.

The problem which this system failed to tackle was that of the polluter not paying - the major users of the roads in a parish were not the inhabitants, but rather those passing through often with heavy loads for markets in other places. Their contribution to the effort of repair was made in their own parish and was but a fraction in recompense for the wear and tear they inflicted on the roads in general. The problem of selfish interest therefore remained during a period of increasing trade in the seventeenth century and was not helped by the unwillingness of labourers (one volunteer being worth ten pressed men) nor by Surveyors whose unpaid posts were held on an annual basis and led to low levels of skill and little continuity of effort.

New Bridges,
St Ives
photo: polystar

1.3 Available Technology

At the end of the seventeenth century in archaeological terms, the Iron Age was still very much in progress with timber, fired clay, stone and metal being the major materials for any significant undertaking. Power was sourced from either muscle, wind or water, all three being used in the various forms of mills at fixed locations, the former two for locomotion on land or water. The wonders of steam that could turn heat into motion were as yet unheard of and the nation's wealth was traded and defended by sailing ships of timber, tar and hemp rope.

The transportation of goods thus involved considerable effort and consequently costs away from the cheapest place of production rose sharply. A number of rivers had been made navigable but significant areas remained beyond the reach of water-borne transport. The roads thus acted as both feeders to the river system and as the main means of transport where the rivers did not reach. In addition some goods did not travel well by water, others might not risk military intervention at sea whilst even more were better walking themselves to market. Whilst road transport was many times more expensive per ton per mile, the differential being relatively less for more expensive goods, it was often the preferred alternative.

There was a large network of 'carriers' operating around the country, usually based at various inns and for the most part employing packhorses. The seventeenth century saw these augmented by increasing amounts of wheeled transport, largely as a result of the increasing size and quantity of goods being traded, which led ultimately to a renewed crisis on the roads. A response to this were the various 'Wheel Acts' which sought to limit the damage to the roads by legislating about permissible loads and wheel widths. These were doomed to failure as essentially against the spirit of the times they tried to contain the damage with preventative measures.

And whereas the Wheels of many Carts, Carrs, and Brewers Drays, now commonly used for the Carriage of Goods, Beer, Ale, and other things, from place to place within the Cities of London and Westminster, and Parishes aforesaid, where the Streets are Paved, are made thinner or narrower in the Felleys then formerly, and many are Shod with Iron Tyres, by means whereof the Pavements in the Streets of the said Cities and Places are daily impaired and broken up, and made dirty and rough: For prevention whereof for the time to come, Be it therefore Enacted by the Authority aforesaid, That from and after the Fifteenth day of December, the Wheels of every Cart, Carr or Dray to be used for the Carriage of any thing whatsoever, from any place within the said Cities and Places, to any place situate in the said Cities and Places where the Streets are Paved, shall be made to contain the full breadth of Six Inches in the Felley, and shall not be wrought about with any Iron Work whatsoever, nor be drawn with above the number of two Horses, after they are up the Hills from the Water-side; And the Owners and Pro=

Extract from London Wheel Act, 1690 (from Searle - 1930)

1.4 Justice Trusts

The parish repair system had taken each parish's previous Common Law obligation to maintain local roads and enshrined it in national legislation which was not in fact abolished until the General Highway Act of 1835. The system contained no requirement for the improvement of roads to cater for increased usage and was essentially an evenly applied remedy to a very uneven problem. Considerable differences existed between parishes both in terms of size and the numbers of roads to repair, population density and availability of labour and local geology which affected both the quality of substrate and availability of materials for repair. A further overlay of differing amounts of road usage near towns as trade increased and carriers turned to waggons and coaches led to a result that included many extremes.

In some parishes the roads were doubtless adequate whilst in others they were difficult to start with, poorly repaired and subject to increasingly heavy usage. This final straw was the key to a solution, the earliest tolls levied to pay for repair being those charged by the Justice trusts of the late seventeenth century. The first of these dates from 1663 and was set up to remedy problems on part of the Great North Road, particularly where it crosses modern Cambridgeshire and where the Justices had previously tried all else at their disposal without success.

The concept of tolls was not new and had in the past been used to fund both 'pavage' and 'pontage' as well as to recoup costs for occasional private roads. It was therefore no great leap to apply such a toll to remedy a problem on a particular public road, the Justices retaining control of both the tolled road and the others within a parish.

A further twelve Justice trusts were set up on particularly bad roads between 1696 and 1714 by which time the turnpike trust proper was beginning to emerge as a more suitable vehicle for setting the roads to rights.

Wansford Bridge,
River Nene
photo: polystar

1.5 Turnpike Trusts

The earliest turnpike trusts date from 1707 and, although still under the control of the Justices who were usually included amongst their number anyway, were run by trustees who were able to spread the administrative load of managing the roads which was threatening to swamp the Justices' other duties. The trusts were composed for the most part of local gentlemen and landowners, who as trustees were not able to profit from the trust itself. They could however foresee the relief afforded to their parishes by the indirect benefits of improved local economies that would ensue from making outsiders pay for the maintenance of the local roads.

Turnpike trusts were but one of many types of local 'ad hoc' body set up during the eighteenth century amongst which are included the Incorporated Guardians of the Poor. These latter set up 'Unions' of several parishes to build a workhouse, which could then be let as a going concern to a local manufacturer who would feed the occupants in return for the use of their labour, thus relieving the parishes of the burden of the poor. These were as much forerunners of local authority Social Services departments as the turnpike trusts were of Highways departments, both marking the beginnings of bringing various systems into public control, without incurring great expense.

It should be remembered that the turnpike trusts were no more than non profit making trusts set up to manage existing routes, very unlike the later canal and railway concerns which were joint stock companies with shareholders whose aim was to create new routes and make money. Each turnpike trust was set up by an Act of Parliament, usually following vigorous petitioning by local worthies about the state of the roads. Parliamentary permission was necessary because the enterprise required the extinction of the former communal right of free passage and it became usual for Acts to last for a period of twenty one years, although renewal was usually forthcoming.

Anno XV.

Caroli II. Regis.

An Act for Repairing
the High-ways within the Counties of *Hertford*, *Cambridge* and *Huntington*.

 Whereas the ancient high-way and Post-Road leading from London to York, and so into Scotland, and likewise from London into Lincolnshire, lieth for many miles in the Counties of Hertford, Cambridge and Huntington, in many of which places the Road, by reason of the great and many Loads which are weekly drawn in Waggons through the said places, as well by reason of the great Trade of Barley and Mault that cometh

Extract from First Turnpike Act, 1663
(from Searle - 1930)

8

1.6 Turnpike Mania

In the years up to 1750 some 133 turnpike trusts received their Acts of Parliament and roads were turnpiked in two main areas. Firstly, and mainly before 1720, the network of radial roads emanating from London were covered by a number of linear trusts, each one's territory abutting the next.

This process continued in the following thirty years alongside the second concentration of town-centred trusts which developed along the Severn valley between Bristol (at that time England's second largest city) and a rapidly developing Birmingham. Around mid-century the turnpike idea seems to have captured the imagination in a big way and between 1751 and 1772 a further 418 Acts were passed, which effectively allowed the turnpike system to cover the country.

The uncertainties that led up to the American War of Independence brought this age of confidence to a sudden halt in 1773 and the ensuing years that also included the Napoleonic Wars saw greatly reduced activity in terms of new trusts. A further 400 or so trusts were set up between 1773 and 1836 of which 59 alone were in the years 1824 to 1826.

These later years of lesser activity were due in part to a saturation point being reached but should also be seen against the beginnings of the years of the boom in canal building from 1770 along with the industrial revolution getting into full swing, doubtless helped along its way by the greatly improved transport, trade and communications links provided by the turnpikes. The final mini-boom in turnpike activity of 1824 to 1826, probably represents a mopping up of the last remaining suitable routes in slightly improved times. Whilst Acts continued to be renewed throughout most of the nineteenth century, the last new Act of 1836 foreshadows the coming of the railways in the 1840's and the growing realisation that the days of the turnpikes were numbered.

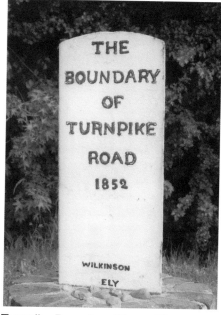

Turnpike Boundary Stone, Ely
(Cambridge - Ely etc.)
photo: polystar

MELTON.

MESSRS. LENNY AND SMITH

Are honored with instructions from the Trustees of the Ipswich and Southtown Turnpike, to Sell by Auction,

AT THE COACH AND HORSES INN, MELTON,

ON

Monday next, October 28th, 1872

AT TWO O'CLOCK PRECISELY,

The undermentioned Valuable Properties, in Lots under such Conditions as will then and there be produced.

NAMELY. LOT I.--The substantially erected

FREEHOLD BUILDING CALLED MELTON

TOLL HOUSE

with Shed for water carts & tools, & a large piece of excellent garden ground having a frontage upon the Main Road of about 160 feet, & another upon the Asylum Road of about 126 feet; also the toll gate & posts. LOT 2.—The materials of the Toll House at Rushmere, with the gate & posts. LOT 3.—The side gate & posts with Keepers' Hut at Kesgrave. LOT 4.—Water Cart. LOT 5.—Ditto. LOT 6.—Ditto. LOT 7.—Snow plough. LOT 8.—Wheelbarrow. LOT 9.—Ditto. LOT 10.—Ditto. LOT 11.—Ditto. LOT 12.—Pick and three stone hammers. LOT 13.—Ditto. LOT 14.—Brush bill, adze and hoe. LOT 15.—Ditto. LOT 16.—Rake and sieve. LOT 17.—Three hoes and three hammers. Also if not previously disposed of by private contract. LOT 18.—An iron pump on Rushmere Heath. LOT 19.—Ditto at Playford. LOT 20.—Two iron pumps at Kesgrave. LOT 21.—An Iron Pump at Martlesham. LOT 22.—An Iron Pump at Woodbridge. LOT 23.—Ditto at Woodbridge (near the nursery). LOT 24.—An iron pump at Melton. LOT 25.—Ditto at Melton, (next the Parish Land). LOT 26.—Ditto at Melton, (next the property of JAMES PACKE ESQ.) LOT 27.—An iron pump at Ufford. LOT 28.—Ditto at Petistree. LOT 29.—Ditto against the County Bridge at Wickham Market.

Further information may be obtained of R. B. Baas, Esq., Solicitor, and of the Auctioneers, Halesworth.

S. B. FYFE, PRINTER, HALESWORTH.

Toll-house Sale Poster, 1872
(from Serjeant & Penrose - 1973)

10

1.7 Winding Up

By the 1840's the turnpike road system had reached its greatest extent with over 20,000 miles of road under the control of over a thousand trusts. During the preceding century the growth and improvement of the system had greatly reduced travelling times and consequently enlarged the market place. Road construction techniques had gradually improved from the early days of simply piling another layer of gravel on top to the latter years, under the influence of great engineers like Telford or McAdam, when roads were rebuilt with a firm foundation and progressively smaller sized stones rolled in, to provide a freely draining cambered finish.

Inland transportation as a whole, with the complementary system of canals, had been greatly improved but not revolutionised, as it was still essentially bound by the limitations of muscle and wind power. It was the magic of steam in the form of the railways which ultimately brought the revolution. The turnpike system suffered first followed by the canals, as both were swept away as passengers and then freight took to the rails.

The turnpike trusts were thus subjected to falling receipts through the mid-nineteenth century which made it increasingly difficult for them to deliver the goods.

Lack of repairs led to a growing resentment to their charges amongst their customers, perhaps most strongly felt in Wales where the 'Rebecca' Riots of the 1840's saw the destruction of many gates and toll-houses by men disguised in female clothing, in imitation of the biblical Rebecca and her daughters.

By the 1870's the trusts were being wound up, their assets in the form of toll-houses and equipment were sold off, and the responsibility for the roads, which they still did not own, vested in the Highway Boards, forerunners of the County Councils.

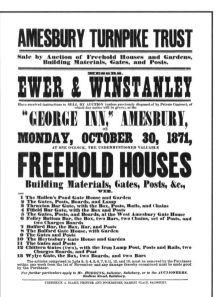

Toll-house Sale Poster, 1871
(from Wright - 1992)

2.0 Collecting the Tolls

Toll Gate Collection
(from Smith - 1970)

A TABLE of the TOLLS payable at this TURNPIKE GATE.
[By the Local Act.]

s d

FOR every Horse.Mule.Afs.or other Beast (Except Dogs) drawing any Coach.Berlin.Landau.Barouche.Chariot.Chaise.Chair.Hearse. Gig.Curricle.Whiskey.Taxed Cart.Waggon.Wain.Timber frame.Cart frame Dray or other Vehicle of whatsoever description when drawn by more than one Horse or other Beast the Sum of Four pence half-penny Such Waggon.Wain.Cart.or other such Carriage having Wheels of lefs breadth than four and a half inches _____ " 4½

AND when drawn by one Horse or other Beast only the sum of six pence (Waggons.Wains and other such Carriages having Wheels as aforesaid) " 6

FOR every Dog drawing any Truck.Barrow or other Carriage for the space of One Hundred Yards or upwards upon any part of the said Roads. the Sum of One Penny _____ " 1

FOR every Horse.Mule.Afs.or other Beast laden or unladen and not drawing. the Sum of Two-pence _____ " 2

FOR every carriage moved or propelled by Steam or Machinery or by any other power than Animal power the Sum of one Shilling for each Wheel thereof _____ 1 0

FOR every Score of Oxen.Cows or neat Cattle.the Sum of Ten-pence and so in Proportion for any greater or lefs Number _____ " 10

FOR every Score of Calves.Sheep.Lambs or Swine the Sum of Five pence and so in proportion for any greater or lefs Number _____ " 5

(By 4.G. 4.C.95)

FOR every Horse.Mule.Afs or other Beast drawing any Waggon Wain.Cart or other such Carriage having the Fellies of the Wheels of the breadth of Six Inches or upwards at the Bottom when drawn by more than one Horse.Mule.Afs or other Beast the Sum of Three-pence " 3

AND when drawn by one Horse.Mule.Afs or other Beast the Sum of Four-Pence (Except Carts) _____ " 4

FOR every Horse.Mule.Afs or other Beast drawing any Waggon Wain.Cart or other such Carriage having the Fellies of the Wheels of the Breadth of four inches and a half and lefs than Six inches when drawn by more than one Horse.Mule.Afs or other Beast the Sum of Three-pence three farthings _____ " 3¾

AND when drawn by one Horse.Mule.Afs or other Beast the Sum of Five-pence (Except Carts) _____ " 5

FOR every Horse.Mule.Afs or other Beast drawing any Cart with Wheels of every Breadth when drawn by only one such Animal the Sum of Six Pence _____ " 6

NB Two Oxen or neat Cattle drawing shall be considered as one Horse 3.G.4.C.126.

CARRIAGES with four Wheels affixed to any Waggon or Cart all as if drawn by two Horses. Carriages with two Wheels so d pay Toll as if drawn by one Horse but such Carriages are Tolls if conveying any Goods other than for Protection.

Toll Board from Sussex
(from Harris - no date)

2.1 Toll Gates & Turnpikes

The turnpike trusts were generally empowered by their Acts of Parliament to 'erect or cause to be erected a gate or gates, turnpike or turnpikes', usually in positions that were left to their own discretion. Certain towns did lobby Parliament and as a result toll gates could not be placed nearer than three miles distant so as not to discourage local markets. Trusts with linear routes therefore tended to have toll gates at either end of their territory with occasional others inbetween, often where a side road joined the way. In contrast the town-centred trusts tended to end up with a ring of toll gates around the outskirts guarding virtually every road inwards.

The trusts were however compelled to enforce a strictly defined set of toll charges that were to a large degree proportional to the amounts of damage caused by differing types of traffic. Local traffic was often favoured by being allowed a same day return trip at no extra cost and there were a number of common exemptions from toll, notably people going to church or to vote, agricultural traffic, the Army and mail coaches which sounded their horns on approaching the gates.

Most trusts had three main employees: a surveyor to initiate and oversee repairs together with a clerk and treasurer to administer their affairs. Their tasks were to engage labour as required to mend the roads and oversee the collectors employed at each toll gate. There was an inherent weak link in the system here that depended on the honesty of the collectors or pike-men as they became known. This led in due course to the practice of toll farming, whereby the proceeds of a toll gate for the coming year were sold off by auction to 'toll farmers', either individual collectors with initiative, or contractors who took on themselves the risk of employing several collectors. The trusts were thus assured of a toll income, which was often supplemented by composition payments from parishes who bought themselves out of their statutory labour obligations.

Toll Farming Poster, 1862
(from Serjeant & Penrose - 1973)

2.2 Toll-houses

To facilitate the twenty four hour presence of their collectors, the turnpike trusts usually built small associated dwellings at their gates:- the toll-houses. They generally comprised very minimal accommodation of two rooms with a scullery and privy attached, although larger types did become more common in later years. The larger ones were probably the result of toll-farming, the houses being bid for at auction both as generators of toll income and as accommodation for the pike-men. These toll-houses were either one or two storeyed and thus came in many shapes and sizes, some trusts adopting a standard design whilst others seem to have tried many variations.

If built to a normal rectangular plan they would often have gable windows very close to the front corner of the building or a bay window on the main room to provide the collector with a view up and down the road. A development of the bay came in the form of the octagonal ended house where effectively the bay became the room, this particular form becoming the norm for the toll-house building-type to such an extent that it was also employed at toll collection points on the canals. The octagonal shape also appears in some country house park gatekeeper's lodges, where again an element of control was required.

It may thus have its roots in the neo-classical love of geometry or possibly may be derived from military precedents of a defensive nature, as many toll-houses of the more ornate 'gothick' kind sport the mock battlements of the picturesque. Wherever the shape derived from, it was nevertheless of great utility.

Much can be said for the presence of the buildings themselves; their many windows and forward position would undoubtedly have unsettled any approaching traveller intent on avoiding the toll with a feeling of having his every move watched. It is this presence that remains today as such a helpful clue to identifying toll-houses, particularly when they are not of the obvious octagonal type.

Porch and Window, Wintringham (*St Neots - Cambridge*)
photo: polystar

15

Whilst the pikeman's job required his presence on the premises it was not strictly necessary for him to be on guard looking out of the windows twenty four hours of the day. Most toll-houses were built on very small parcels of land owned by the trustees, usually carved out of the corners of fields, but sufficient to allow the tenants a small cottage garden for their home grown produce. Because of their usual remoteness these small plots often also contained their own well or pump for water supply.

Internally the toll-houses would have been very cramped by modern day standards, particularly if the pike-man had a family of any size. The small bedroom would have slept the whole family, a truckle bed for the children sliding out from beneath the main one, as can be seen at the Sussex toll-house at the Weald and Downland Museum. The other room served every other purpose, being in every sense the living room, and contained the hearth where food was cooked, together with seating, tables, storage etc. and may well have been awkward to furnish if without any square corners at all. The main door to the highway usually led off this room and it was often protected by a porch or shelter of some kind where the collector could receive tolls in the dry.

Another common indicative feature of toll-houses is a blanked out window at first floor level where a toll board would have been placed. Sited as they were hard against the highway, those that survive today are perhaps the most visible remains of the turnpike system. The keen industrial archaeologist will also be able to find many examples of contemporary milestones, a later requirement of the turnpike legislation, as most of the roads today that show 'MS' at one mile intervals on Ordnance Survey maps were originally turnpike roads. There are also a few surviving gates, their general form consisting of a main vehicular gate or turnpike (originally a spiked pole) across the road, with usually a pedestrian gate between this and the toll-house.

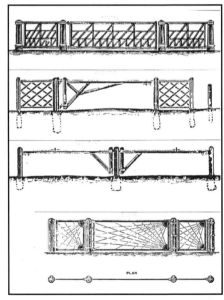

Varieties of Toll Gate
(from Searle - 1930)

2.3 Local Distinctiveness

A particular problem with toll-houses is dating their construction. In between a *terminus post quem* of the original turnpike act and a *terminus ante quem* of finding them on a tithe map or early Ordnance Survey lie many years. Most will be found to have been constructed nearer the earlier date at the beginning of a turnpike's existence and therefore not benefiting from the slightly improved communications that followed by overland transport. They were even less likely to have benefited from the greater improvements that the canals later brought to water borne transport, and certainly missed out on the radically changed face of building material distribution ushered in by the railway age.

In terms of their walling materials therefore, toll-houses were almost universally built of what was locally available and remain to this day useful pointers to local distinctiveness and the nature of the geology thereabouts. Thus in Plymouth we find the local Devonian limestone used (see below), in Bath an Oolitic limestone, in Anglesey the local metamorphic rock and at Todmorden, in the Pennines, Millstone Grit. As eighteenth century buildings, where stone was not available, brick was usually the order of the day, so that in Cambridge we find white Gault Clay bricks (see p.1), whilst in Essex red brick and tile from the London Clay.

Local Devonian Limestone Toll-house in Plymouth
(from Searle - 1930)

Although the timber-frame tradition had long gone into decline, and certainly was less suitable for forming an octagonal building, there is a timber-framed toll-house in Suffolk, and the lap-boarded Sussex example in the Weald and Downland Museum, both of which are rectangular in plan.

Roofing materials show a similar pattern. Thatch was the material of an earlier age and unsuitable anyway as it represented a severe fire risk, should there be any local dissent about the coming of the turnpikes. Pantiles and the larger stone flags and tiles, whilst not best suited to the small areas of hipped roofs involved in octagonal buildings, were sometimes used nevertheless, more so on the rectangular examples. Slate, however, was the new material of the age and seems to have been the predominant choice, even in the east where it had to be imported from afar. In the eighteenth century roofs were generally pitched according to the materials used, a slate or pantile roof requiring less timber at 30° to 40° pitch, than would a plaintile roof at 45° or more. The presence of a steep slate roof therefore often suggests a replacement covering to an earlier roof.

We have seen that toll-houses were basic small domestic buildings, housing persons fairly low down the social scale. As such they fit within the vernacular tradition, although the tendency has been for them to be studied as curiosities within the province of the industrial archaeologist. Within this vernacular tradition they may be considered somewhere near its later threshold, as particularly with the octagonal forms, there is an overlay of the 'polite', a signalling of their purpose as a particular type of building. This is especially true where a standard design marks their belonging to a particular trust or they venture into the 'picturesque' at the whim of the trustees. The fashionable input could manifest itself as 'gothick' windows or even crenellated parapets, which by this time presumably no longer required the King's licence.

These fashions were however directed from above, being very much the prerogative of the trustees, who as fashionable members of the gentry would have been very aware of the latest ideas and as keen to try them out on their turnpike roads as at their lodge gates. It is therefore possible that the octagonal form used in toll-houses derived from earlier garden buildings of this shape, as is believed to have happened with park lodge gatehouses. The turnpike roads can be seen in this light as a parallel phenomenon to the enclosures and creation of our country house estates. The gentry not only came to control large areas of land, signalling this benign stewardship with their various gatekeeper's lodges, but also the routes between the major centres, controlled by the toll-houses.

18

2.4 What Lies Ahead?

Local distinctiveness relates to the customs and ways of doing things that have evolved in an area, and which give it a distinctive local character. This 'difference from other places' appears not only in the landscape moulded by our management of the land but also in our built environment. An important part of maintaining local distinctiveness therefore involves celebrating the differences, keeping alive the stories and associations of a place.

The problem with toll-houses in this respect is their situation. They were mostly built in isolation, on the perimeters of our settlements and as a consequence almost never occur within our historic centres, where most modern day celebration of place happens. Whilst the turnpikes probably initiated ribbon development, encouraging the spread of suburban villas, their remains are now largely surrounded by it, so that apart from their intimate link with the actual road, toll-houses have little sense of place.

Unfortunately the road itself has become too fast and dangerous a place to encourage anyone to stop and wonder. Meanwhile our canals and railways, which move at a more human pace, have become the subjects of the majority of transport nostalgia, and thus leisure activity.

The major residual usage of toll-houses is as dwellings and as such they are cramped and therefore often extended; they are poorly serviced because of their remoteness and often unpleasantly sited on the highway edge. We therefore find our remaining toll-houses the unconsidered remnants of a forgotten system, infrequently listed unless tending towards the more 'polite' and severely at risk from future road developments.

In order to celebrate what is left, we need to take the first step in recognising it. Accordingly we will now look at Cambridgeshire's turnpike roads and toll-houses in greater detail.

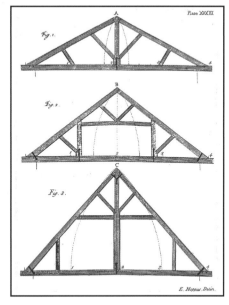

Varieties of Roof Pitch for Different Roofing Materials (from Cruickshank & Wyld - 1975)

19

3.0 The Cambridgeshire Turnpikes

Stagecoach and Four
(from Smith - 1970)

photo: stretham engine trust

Toll-board from Stretham Engine Toll-house (Stoker's Cottage)

Transcript:

WATERBEACH LEVEL BANK TOLLS PAYABLE HERE	
For Every Horse or other Beast except an ass or asses hauling any boat or boats	1/4d
For every ass hauling	4d
For every horse mule ass not hauling any vessel	1½d
For every score of neat cattle	1/3d
But if under five for each beast	1d
For every score of calves swine sheep or lambs	10d
and so in proportion for any greater or lesser number	
T. MUSGRAVE FRANCIS Clerk to the Commissioners	

3.1 Cambridgeshire Turnpike Trusts

Compared to other counties, modern Cambridgeshire has effectively two counties' worth of trusts. The area was very much at the forefront of turnpike activity, with the majority of its roads that were turnpiked, achieving that status by the end of the boom of the 1760's. Proximity to London is one main factor in this, the Great North Road in particular being a major radial route for trade. The Wadesmill to Stilton section was turnpiked by the first ever Justice trust in 1663, the renewal in 1710 covering Royston to Wansford Bridge, this road essentially taking a major south-north route across the difficult Oxford Clay.

Further connections into the county from the south were made in 1724 by a trust covering the Chesterford to Cambridge and Newmarket roads. These were essentially continuations northwards from Stump Cross of an Essex road that by 1702 had been turnpiked as far north as Harlow. From these two tentative starts the rest of the system was to grow. In 1725 the Trumpington to Fowlmere Trust covered the road southwards out of Cambridge off the Chesterford road. The same year another south-north route was introduced from Biggleswade in Bedfordshire up to Alconbury on the Great North Road. Next there came some necessary improvements to fenland roads, with Chatteris to Somersham in 1728 and Wisbech to March in 1730.

In 1745, after a few years of relative inactivity, further links were made into Cambridge itself with the Godmanchester to Newmarket Heath road passing through the city. The Great North Road was extended in 1750 with a branch from Stilton into Peterborough and then with new trusts covering from Brampton westwards to Market Harborough in 1752 and from Alconbury to Oundle in 1753. Links were then made westwards to Wellingborough in Northamptonshire with trusts for roads south-westwards out of Peterborough via Oundle in 1754 and north-westwards from Great Staughton in 1755.

Milestone, Lincoln Road, Peterborough
photo: polystar

1755 also saw the turnpiking of two roads southwards out of Ramsey, one to Huntingdon, the other from Bury, just south of Ramsey, via St Ives and then all the way south to Stratton near Biggleswade. The Cambridge to Ely and Soham road was turnpiked in 1763, and then extended to Littleport in 1765 and to Mepal and Downham Market in 1770. Meanwhile the Great North Road was extended beyond Huntingdon to Somersham in 1765. That same year the Chatteris to Somersham road was extended to St Ives and thence east to Earith, and the Wisbech to March road was extended to Chatteris. The fens were finally connected by road to the rest of the county as they were to Norfolk by the Wisbech to South Lynn road also of 1765.

There was also intensive activity in the south at this time with the Haverhill to Shelford Trust providing a link into Cambridge from the south-east in 1766 and the Tring to Bourn Bridge road crossing the south of the county in 1769. 1770 saw the Biggleswade to Alconbury road given a branch across to St Neots, and in 1772 new trusts linked Chatteris to Ramsey and Cambridge to St Neots. After a gap of twenty years, the road was turnpiked to Thorney, east of Peterborough in 1792, the link onwards to Wisbech not coming until a further trust was set up in 1810.

Cambridge was connected to Royston in 1793 and to Arrington Bridge on the Great North Road in 1797, this road being extended by another trust onwards to Potton in 1826. Meanwhile Potton had been connected to St Neots in 1814.

Whilst all these turnpike trusts were being established, there was other traffic around the county that eventually became liable for tolls. The many Drainage Boards that maintained the fenland rivers were empowered by Acts of Parliament to collect tolls from those using the drover's routes to pay for the maintenance of the river banks, one such act in 1797 being for the Waterbeach Level (see p.21).

Godmanchester Turnpike Stone, Cambridge
photo: polystar

23

3.2 Limestone and Clay

The oldest rocks of greater Cambridgeshire are those of the far north-west where Jurassic limestones of the Great Oolite, some 200 million years old, form a ridge through Rockingham Forest to the west of Peterborough. This is essentially the north-eastern extension of the Cotswolds and here divides the drainage of the Lincolnshire River Welland to the north, from that of the Cambridgeshire River Nene to the south, passing through both Peterborough and Wisbech.

In their lower reaches both these rivers and the Great Ouse pass through Fenland, recent alluvial deposits of peat, which obscure the older geology below. Much of this fertile new land is the product of the drainage schemes of the seventeenth century, which contained these rivers and fed them in a more orderly fashion to their outlets in The Wash.

South-east of the limestone ridge there is a thicker band of later and softer Jurassic rocks, the Oxford Clays belonging to the Middle Oolite series. This presents us with a low lying plain some twenty miles wide that dips north-east of Ramsey below the obscuring Fenland deposits. Within this plain are the settlements of Stilton, Kimbolton, Huntingdon, St Ives and St Neots.

Moving further south-east we come to the younger rocks of the Upper Oolite, continuing in alternating bands of limestone and clay. First come the Corallian beds running from Eltisley, west of Cambridge, to March in the north (here not notably limestone with fossil corals except at an outlier near Upware north-east of Cambridge). Next in the succession is the Kimmeridge Clay, our youngest Jurassic rocks some 150 million years old, their greatest extent here being a large area around Ely.

Ely itself is on a smaller island above the Kimmeridge Clay of Lower Greensand, the earliest rocks of the Cretaceous, which run in another low ridge south-west to north-east across the county and onwards into the west of Norfolk. Above this another softer belt of Gault Clay forms an extensive lowland area around Cambridge and Soham. This is capped in turn by a very thin layer of Upper Greensand, containing fossils and coprolites, phosphatic nodules which were mined for use as fertiliser.

These all give way further east to the ubiquitous Chalk that runs on out of the county into Norfolk, Suffolk and north Essex. Here it forms a low escarpment including the Gog Magog Hills just south-east of Cambridge, but further south-west it becomes the more impressive ridge of the Chilterns.

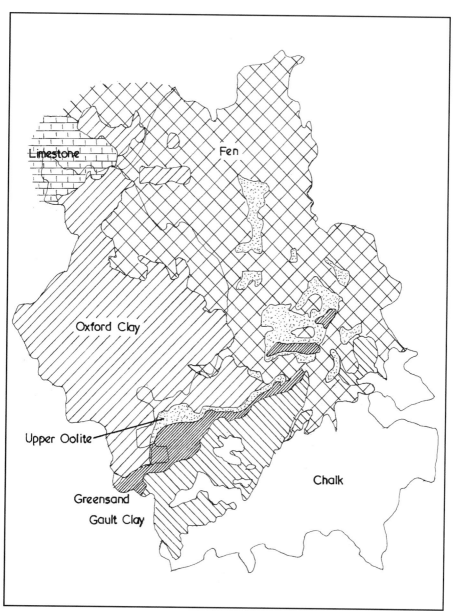

The Geology of Cambridgeshire

3.3 Timber, Brick and Tile

The chalkland part of our area's south-eastern corner is very much like its continuation into the adjoining counties, although here the chalk is more elevated and less covered by later deposits so that it looks more like the chalk downlands found further south-west.

The local vernacular here is also like that of the adjoining counties, mostly a timber-framed tradition with rendered walls and thatched roofs, with the usual later burnt clay materials such as brick and plaintile in evidence too, where new fronts and re-roofing have been undertaken.

The chalk itself was used as a building stone where it was hard enough, the now defunct quarry at Burwell being the last source of 'clunch' to close. The chalk also produced flints, which can be seen in many of the local churches, and mixed with clay the raw material for a type of 'clay lump'.

West of the chalk, the low lying areas around Cambridge see a preponderance of the white brick made from the local Gault Clays, relatively high in calcium carbonate content. Within Cambridge itself, this is augmented by much imported stone that the city's wealth was able to command. Many of the colleges are built using Barnack stone from just west of Peterborough.

Immediately below the Gault Clay, the Lower Greensand provided Carstone, a hard ferruginous sandstone more prevalent in north-west Norfolk around Downham Market, but at one time quarried near Ely.

The local limestone from the Corallian beds further north-west of Cambridge was a little used locally but either side the Kimmeridge and Oxford clays return us to brick country. These bricks are mostly red in colour, but can be of a rather unremarkable dull pinkish tinge, somewhere between red and white. Indeed the modern day 'common' brick is one such, mass produced from huge industrialised claypits dug into the Oxford Clay around Fletton, south of Peterborough.

Ely, Huntingdon and St Ives sit within the clay country, but with their relative wealth provide further small oases of imported stone on the grander buildings. This stone came across the fens by boat, mainly from the far north-west of our area, where we find true limestone country, where the stone is used both for walls and as slates for roofs.

3.4 Cambridgeshire Toll-houses

The majority of surviving toll-houses in greater Cambridgeshire are of rectangular plan, but within that generalisation they are all different, no standard plans having been adopted. The larger foursquare two storey examples are mainly in the fens, with good examples at Littleport, Witcham, Chatteris (Tuck's Gate) and Wisbech (Lynn Road), all having certain similarities. Other two storey toll-houses provide more variety such as the hipped slate roof at Elm Road, Wisbech and the mansard plaintile roof at Godmanchester, both of these with first floor side windows.

The single storey examples are even more varied. Hipped roofs with a central projecting bay are found at Nene Way and Horsey, and with a small porch at Wintringham. Croydon has a hipped slate roof with no projections. Otherwise we find gabled roofs with the gable facing the road as in the lost example at Sutton (Beds) or more often with the ridge parallel to the road. Variety is shown here with the materials used such as limestone and pantile at Elton, brick and slate at Croydon (now rendered over) or rendered timber frame and thatch at Abington.

As has been seen with the other eastern counties covered by this series of books, toll-houses with octagonal ends or bays are not the norm in this part of the world. Greater Cambridgeshire presents us with just four surviving examples, all in brick (one rendered over). Two are of two storeys at Keyston and Trumpington, two of one storey at Pickle Fen and Paper Mill, Cambridge. These are all of Victorian date with slate roofs and seem to have used the octagonal form to signal their purpose.

Carstone, White Brick and Slate
Ring's End, Guyhirn
photo: polystar

As a result of this, after the following gazetteer section describing the county's toll-houses, there will be found an appendix illustrating other octagonal buildings around the county - they do exist, it is just that they are not toll-houses.

4.0 A Cambridgeshire Gazetteer

The remainder of this book comprises a gazetteer of both toll-houses and their former sites. In general all surviving toll-houses are illustrated and given a map reference without brackets. Those that have been lost, but where a suitable photograph has been forthcoming, are also illustrated but given bracketed references. The remaining toll-house sites, lost completely without trace other than documentary, are described as far as possible in the boxes at the foot of each page. Those that appeared as 'T.B.' on Charles and John Greenwoods' map of 1834 or 'T.G.' and 'T.P.' on the first edition Ordnance Survey maps of c.1838 are so marked.

The gazetteer starts in the far north-east of the county with the Isle of Ely adjoining Norfolk, runs westwards towards Peterborough and then south through Huntingdonshire and finally east to the area around Cambridge with its links into Suffolk. Purists may question the validity of including a few from just into adjoining counties, but they are there for completeness; no county stands alone. The author is very conscious of this being a first attempt to document these buildings in such detail and would be very grateful to hear of any errors, omissions, additional information or photographic evidence in respect of any toll-house that readers might be aware of.

Readers should be aware that most of our surviving toll-houses are now in private ownership as people's homes, please respect this. The author apologises in advance to any owners for any nuisance this publication might bring their way, and hopes the benefits of wider knowledge of this obscure subject can be seen to outweigh any inconvenience caused.

It is certainly hoped that a good many owners will come to appreciate their guardianship of this small part of our heritage, and perhaps a few more of these unique buildings will in due course get the added protection of becoming listed buildings, rather than become the subjects of memorials like the adjoining illustration.

Memorial Stone for Burwell Ness Toll-house, Cambridgeshire
photo: polystar

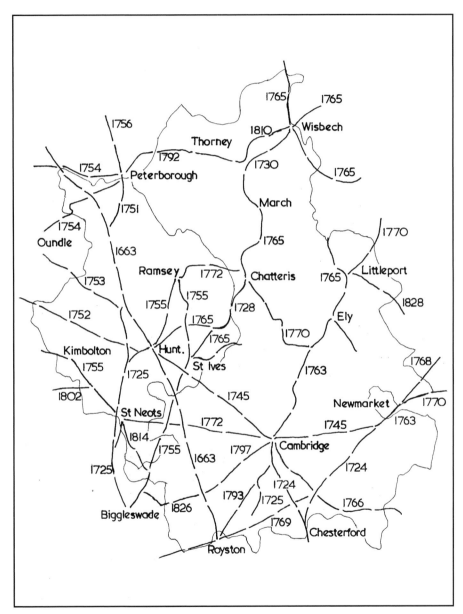

The Main Turnpike Roads of Cambridgeshire

Date	Act	Turnpike
1663	15 CII c.1	Royston - Wansford Bridge
1724	10 GI c.12	Chesterford - Newmarket Heath & Cambridge
1725	11 GI c.14	Fowlmere - Trumpington
1725	11 GI c.20	Biggleswade - Alconbury etc.
1728	1 GII (2) c.4	Chatteris Ferry - Somersham
1730	3 GII c.24	Wisbech - March
1745	18 GII c.23	Godmanchester - Cambridge - Newmarket Heath
1751	24 GII c.59	Stilton - Peterborough (+)
1752	25 GII c.57	Market Harborough - Brampton etc.
1753	26 GII c.88	Oundle - Alconbury etc.
1754	27 GII c.23	Peterborough - Oundle - Wellingborough
1754	27 GII c.30	Leicester - Peterborough
1755	28 GII c.26	Ramsey - Huntingdon
1755	28 GII c.33	Great Staughton - Wellingborough etc.
1755	28 GII c.35	Bury (Ramsey) - Stratton (Biggleswade)
1756	29 GII c.85	Lincoln Heath - Peterborough
1763	3 GIII c.32	Newmarket - Newmarket Heath (+)
1763	3 GIII c.36	Cambridge - Ely etc.
1765	5 GIII c.53	Somersham - St Ives - Earith (+)
1765	5 GIII c.77	Huntingdon - Somersham (+)
1765	5 GIII c.79	Ely - Littleport & Welney (+)
1765	5 GIII c.83	Chatteris - March, Wisbech - Downham Mkt (+)
1765	5 GIII c.101	Wisbech - South Lynn etc.
1766	6 GIII c.84	Haverhill - Shelford
1768	8 GIII c.55	Thetford - Newmarket
1769	9 GIII c.86	Tring - Bourn Bridge etc.
1770	10 GIII c.96	Bury St Edmunds - Newmarket etc.
1770	10 GIII c.97	Wilburton - Mepal, Littleport - Downham Mkt (+)
1772	12 GIII c.26	Chatteris - Ramsey
1772	12 GIII c.90	St Neots - Cambridge
1792	32 GIII c.129	Peterborough - Thorney
1793	33 GIII c.130	Cambridge - Long Leys & Royston
1797	37 GIII c.179	Cambridge - Arrington Bridge
1802	42 GIII c.64	Great Staughton - Lavendon
1810	50 GIII c.74	Wisbech - Thorney
1814	54 GIII c.180	Potton - Eynesbury (St Neots)
1826	7 GIV c.29	Wimpole (Arrington Bridge) - Potton
1828	9 GIV c.44	Mildenhall - Littleport etc.

The Main Turnpike Trusts of Cambridgeshire
(+) indicates addition to existing trust

Littleport Bridge Toll-house
(TL 578877)   'T.P.'
Mildenhall - Littleport etc

photo: polystar

The turnpike road north-westwards from Mildenhall continues in its flat Fenland manner for about nine miles, crossing the border between Suffolk and Cambridgeshire half-way, eventually reaching the River Great Ouse at Littleport.

Here on the east bank just outside the town, there stood until recently the toll-house that controlled this particular trust's road. By-passed because the road bridge had been moved downstream slightly, it was similar to other toll-houses we will see further into the Isle of Ely.

Brick built, it had a first floor recessed panel (overpainted) for the toll-board and at least one useful small side window.

Washington Toll-house (Norfolk)
(TL 537929)   'Toll Bar'
New Bedford River

The original 1763 road from Cambridge to Ely was extended in 1765 to Littleport and about five miles further north-west to the New Bedford River opposite Welney. Here just into Norfolk at the hamlet of Washington (Suspension Bridge), some form of tolls were collected.

The bridge took the Littleport to Wisbech road over the New River, and on the first edition 1" OS map 'Toll Bar' is shown a short distance along the bank. It therefore seems likely that the tolls were for the drover's road along the river bank, rather than for the turnpike road.

Stretham Toll-house
TL 506746   'T.G.'
Cambridge - Ely etc.

photo: alan rosevear

Just west of the village of Stretham, this toll-house at one time controlled the road towards Wilburton, Haddenham and Witcham, turnpiked as a further extension to the Cambridge to Ely trust's roads in 1770.

West beyond Haddenham the road continues on a causeway across the wetlands of the Lower Delphs to Earith and eventually Huntingdon.

Probably of brick construction, now rendered, it has a plaintile roof with a dormer over a projecting porch. It was shown on the first edition 1" OS map as 'T.G.'

Pyper's Hill Toll-house
(TL 567842)   'T.G.' 'T.B.'
Cambridge - Ely etc.

The other extension of the Cambridge to Ely road in 1770, northwards to Littleport, required a toll-house north of Ely.

Although Greenwood's map of 1834 shows a 'T.B.' at both Chettisham (TL 552836) and Pyper's Hill, it is only the latter that is corroborated by a 'T.G.' on the first edition 1" OS map and the 1839 Littleport tithe map which shows 'Toll Gate' there.

Stretham Engine Toll-house
TL 516729
River Great Ouse

photo: stretham engine trust

This toll-house controlling the south bank of the River Great Ouse, is now known as Stoker's Cottage, on account of its later use in connection with the nearby Stretham Engine, which pumped water out of Stretham Mere.

Tolls were collected from the drovers that used the river bank on behalf of the Waterbeach Level Drainage Commission and presumably used to pay for the upkeep of the banks.

The toll-board from this toll-house (see p.21) is kept in the museum at Stretham Old Engine House. Recently refurbished, the cottage is now managed by the Landmark Trust.

Ely Union Toll-house
(TL 533797)   'T.G.'
Cambridge - Ely etc.

The southern approach to Ely was controlled by a toll-house at a junction just south-west of the town, very near the Union Workhouse. Here the road from Cambridge was joined by that from Chatteris to the west.

The 1846 Ely tithe map shows 'Toll' at this point and the site was shown as 'T.G.' on the first edition 1" OS map.

Waterbeach Toll-house
TL 508658
River Cam

photo: polystar

Known as Garden Tree Gate, this toll-house was probably built in about 1797, when the Waterbeach Level Drainage Commission was first empowered to collect tolls from drovers using the banks of the rivers Great Ouse and Cam.

The river above Bottisham Lock, adjoining this toll-house, was under the control of the Conservators of the River Cam (see p.76).

Originally this toll-house was not unlike that near Stretham Engine House (Stoker's Cottage), but it has now had a first floor added within a slate covered mansard roof.

Soham Toll-house
(TL 489173)   'T.G.'
Cambridge - Ely etc.

The original 1763 turnpike act for the Cambridge to Ely road included a branch south-eastwards from Ely down to Soham.

The toll-house controlling this stretch was built about two miles north-west of Soham. It appeared on the 1845 tithe map as 'Turnpike Gate' and was shown in the apportionment as 'Toll House' owned by 'Trustees of Turnpike Road'.

Earith Toll-house
TL 394745
River Great Ouse

photo: alan rosevear

Very near the Haddenham toll-house controlling the road just east of Earith (see p.38), this one controlled access to the south bank of the River Great Ouse where it diverges from the New Bedford River into its old course via Ely.

Built in a rather curious timber-framed construction with brick infill, it has two ground floor windows and a porch directly facing the former river bank, now the B1050 road south to Willingham, which at its start follows this bank for about a mile to the south-east.

Stretham Ferry Toll-house
(TL 500723) 'T.G.' 'T.B.'
Cambridge - Ely etc.

Further south towards Cambridge there was a toll-house at Stretham Ferry, where what was originally a Roman road crossed the River Great Ouse.

Here the original 1763 turnpike act included for the building of a bridge, on the northern side of which Greenwood (1834) shows 'T.B.' and the first edition 1" OS map shows 'T.G.'

35

Witcham Toll-house

TL 463791   'T.G.'   'T.B.'

Cambridge - Ely etc.

photo: polystar

The Cambridge to Ely Turnpike Trust's roads were further extended in 1770 to another crossing of the New and Old Bedford Rivers at Mepal, the road here leading on to Chatteris.

About two miles before the river crossing, at a cross-roads south of Witcham village, there was a toll-house, which has given its name to the locality as 'Witcham Toll'.

The building shown above is believed to have been the toll-house, one of a pair of buildings here shown on the tithe map of 1841. It is in brick, now rendered, with a blanked out first floor window very similar to that seen at Littleport.

Witcham Hythe Toll-house
(TL 456824)
New Bedford River

Due north of Witcham, on the south bank of the New Bedford River, there was until recently a toll-house used to collect tolls from drovers bringing their animals to market by this route.

The river bank here is straight and uninterrupted for about seven miles to the north-east, where the Washington (Suspension Bridge) toll-house probably served the same function. Further on still was the Salter's Lode toll-house controlling access to the river bank from near Downham Market in Norfolk.

Tucks Gate Toll-house, Chatteris
TL 397854
Cambridge - Ely etc.

photo: polystar

Further along the road through Mepal, on the old road into Chatteris just before a sharp bend this building is also suggestive of being a toll-house.

The western end is obviously an extension, creating a third dwelling in what is now a terrace. The original eastern end seems to have been divided in two and given a new doorway, breaking the former symmetry of the elevation, which up till then would have closely matched the toll-house at Witcham.

The first edition 1" OS map has 'Tucks Gate' inscribed at this point.

> **Mepal Fen Toll-house**
> (TL 436815)
> *Old Bedford River*
>
> Just over the rivers from the village of Mepal, modern maps show 'Toll Farm' indicating some form of collection there, either for use of the road or more likely to catch drovers using the north bank of the Old Bedford River to avoid the toll-house on the south one (see p.36). The Mepal tithe map of 1840 does indeed show two small buildings either side of the road, where the drover's route crossed.
>
> Another 'Toll Farm' about four miles further north-east at TL 461884, a mile south-west of Manea, may refer to this same north bank route.

Ely Road Toll-house, St Ives
(TL 321721)   'T.G.'
Chatteris Ferry - Somersham etc.

photo: huntingdonshire archives

The Chatteris to Somersham turnpike road was extended as far as Sheep Market in St Ives in 1765, and a branch added eastwards serving Earith.

This old photograph shows the toll-house that was built about a mile north-east of the centre of St Ives, where these two roads joined.

Known as 'Republic Cottage' it was shown as 'T.G.' on the first edition 1" OS map and is now the site of a large roundabout.

Haddenham Toll-house, Earith
(TL 395748)   'T.G.'
Chatteris Ferry - Somersham etc.

Two roads from Ely further east feed into the Earith to St Ives road at Haddenham, just east of Earith. Here where the River Great Ouse meets the New Bedford River (or Hundred Foot Drain) there was a toll-house.

It was shown on the first edition 1" OS map as 'T.G.' and the tithe map of 1844 records it as 'Toll Houses and Shed' owned by 'Bedford Level Corporation' and occupied by 'Trustees of Turnpike Road'.

Pickle Fen Toll-house, Chatteris
TL 383832   'T.G.'
Chatteris Ferry - Somersham etc.

photo: polystar

South of Chatteris, the road to Somersham follows the boundary between Huntingdonshire and the Isle of Ely for about four miles.

The road first meets the boundary at Pickle Fen about two miles south of Chatteris, where this unusual not quite octagonal single storey toll-house can be found. It is built in white brick with a slate roof and appears to have been extended by the addition of a similar shaped wing at the rear.

Across the road a grade II listed cast iron milestone exhibiting a cross keys motif records the distances to 'Wisbech 21 Miles' and 'St Ives 10 Miles' (see back cover).

Old Halves Toll-house
(TL 374813)   'T.G.'
Chatteris Ferry - Somersham etc.

This quite early turnpike trust seems to have been set up just for this short section of presumably rather damp road between higher ground at Chatteris and Somersham.

Two miles beyond Pickle Fen, where the road crosses Hammond's Eau, there was also a toll-house at Old Halves. It might be thought that these two sites would duplicate each other, but both sites are shown as 'T.G.' on the first edition 1" OS map and both as 'Toll Bar' on the 1838 Somersham tithe map.

Wimblington Toll-house
TL 413931   'T.P.'   'T.B.'
Chatteris Ferry - Wisbech etc.

photo: alan rosevear

About two miles south of March on the road from Chatteris, there was a toll-house just north of the village of Wimblington. At first inspection this building appears modern with its concrete tiled roof and rendered walls, however where the render is damaged older brickwork can be seen. Its position with a doorway close to the road confirms its former use.

Shown on the 1840 tithe map for the village marked as 'Toll Bar', it is listed in the apportionment as owned by 'Trustees of Wisbeach Turnpike Road'. The 1887 25" first edition OS map shows it as 'Old Toll House', with 'Toll Farm' adjoining it.

Bodsey Toll-house
(TL 294880)   'Toll'
Chatteris - Ramsey

At the southern end of the Chatteris Ferry to Wisbech turnpike road, two miles north of Chatteris itself, a road westwards to Ramsey was the subject of a later turnpike act in 1772, which also involved an element of local drainage works.

The typically straight fenland road ran for about six miles from Carter's Bridge (TL 383885) west to Bodsey Bridge, just beyond which is marked 'Bodsey Toll' on the first edition 1" OS map.

Rings End Toll-house, Guyhirn
TF 398025
River Nene

photo: polystar

South of Guyhirn, the turnpike road from Wisbech heads south away from the river towards March, some five miles distant.

At Rings End a track off the main road is an old drover's route continuing south-west along the south bank of Morton's Leam, which runs parallel to the River Nene.

Access to this was controlled by this octagonal toll-house, built of local carstone with white brick dressings, very like the buildings of Downham Market. It fortunately survives and is now a grade II listed building.

Grandford Toll-house
(TL 394995)   'Toll Bar'
Chatteris Ferry - Wisbech etc.

Roughly midway between Guyhirn and March, there was a toll-house at Grandford, shown as 'Toll Bar' on the first edition 1" OS map.

The March tithe map for the rural area around the town shows little detail of buildings, but there is a small triangular plot on the east side of the road owned by 'Trustees of Wisbeach Turnpike Road'.

Nene Way Toll-house, Guyhirn
TF 405042
River Nene

photo: polystar

This building on the north side of the River Nene north of Guyhirn sits at a junction where the main road veers away from the river north towards Wisbech St Mary.

Here Nene Way continues along the northern river bank, access to which would easily be controlled if this building were a toll-house.

Unfortunately no evidence has been found to show this other than the building being called 'Tollhouse'. However the siting of the porch to the south suggests that it was the river bank that was being controlled here.

Cox's Lane Toll-house, Wisbech
(TF 451086)   'Toll' 'T.B.'
River Nene

The road south-west of Wisbech along the north side of the River Nene had some sort of toll collection at the southern end of Cox's Lane. Nothing appears on the tithe map here, but the first edition 1" OS map has 'Toll' rather than 'T.P.', perhaps indicative of a non-turnpike use.

A toll-house here would have controlled access from the town end onto Nene Way, along the northern river bank.

Elm Road Toll-house, Wisbech
TF 466090   'T.P.'
Chatteris Ferry - Wisbech etc.

photo: polystar

Extensions to the original Wisbech to March road were enacted in 1765 and included roads from Wisbech to Downham Market in Norfolk and Long Sutton in Lincolnshire.

Elm Road out of Wisbech in the direction of Downham Market also had its toll-house, again about half a mile before the road reached into Norfolk, this time south-east of the town centre towards Emneth.

This one with its first floor side window seems to have survived adjoining Elm Road, parallel to the dual carriageway now approaching the town along this route. Again the 1842 tithe map shows both building and bar here, but without further identification.

Sutton Road Toll-house,
(TF 455105)   'T.B.'   **Wisbech**
Chatteris Ferry - Wisbech etc.

The road north-westwards out of Wisbech continued to Tydd Gote and then Long Sutton in Lincolnshire. About a mile from the town centre there was a toll-house where Pickard's Lane joined the main road from the south.

It was shown on both the 1" early OS maps as 'T.B.' and on the 1842 tithe map as 'Toll Gate'.

Outwell Toll-house (Norfolk)
TF 535028
Chatteris Ferry - Wisbech etc.

photo: polystar

On the road from Wisbech towards Downham Market, east of the village of Outwell, this small bungalow goes by the name of 'Tolbar'. The site is further east than early OS maps show ('T.P.' at TF 520037). The building sits hard on the highway edge at a road junction and there was at one time a small gable window on the eastern side, now widened into an internal doorway through to the extension.

About three miles south-west of here at Three Holes there is another 'Toll Bar Cottage' also in Norfolk. This may relate to either the bank of the Middle Level Main Drain or the Littleport to Wisbech road crossing it at Lott's Bridge.

South Side Toll-house, Wisbech
(TF 456093)   'T.B.'
Chatteris Ferry - Wisbech etc.

The original turnpike act of 1730 provided for a road between Wisbech and March, that ran as far as Guyhirn along the south bank of the River Nene. Here just outside the town there was a toll-house guarding the way.

The 1842 tithe map shows both building and bar here, but without further identification. In time the south bank proved difficult to maintain and this particular route had become unsustainable by 1849, when the alternative 'Low Road' via Friday Bridge was turnpiked.

Lynn Road Toll-house, Wisbech
TF 467104   'T.P.'
Wisbech - South Lynn etc.

photo: polystar

The Wisbech to South Lynn turnpike road was part of a much larger trust covering much of the north-west Norfolk fens. The 'Lynn Road' from Wisbech towards Kings Lynn was controlled by this toll-house about half a mile before the Norfolk border, north-east of the town centre, near Walsoken.

The building is of three bays with a central doorway fronting the main road with a blanked out window over for the toll-board. It appeared as 'Toll Gate' on the 1842 Wisbech St Peter tithe map and is built of local dark bricks and now has a replacement concrete tile roof.

Norwich Road Toll-house,
(TF 467096)   'T.P.'   **Wisbech**
Wisbech - South Lynn etc.

About half a mile south of the Lynn Road toll-house, there was another guarding an alternative route out towards Walsoken and the fens east of the town. The roads here would have continued through to Wiggenhall on the west bank of the River Great Ouse.

Like many of the Wisbech toll-houses this one appeared as 'T.P.' on the first edition 1" OS map.

Thorney Toll-house, Thorney Toll
TF 344039   'Toll'
Wisbech - Thorney

photo: polystar

The road westwards from Wisbech to Thorney was not turnpiked until 1810. The western end of this road had a toll-house about four miles east of Thorney at Thorney Toll, a hamlet in its own right.

Now known as 'Toll Cottage', it has been much modernised with a new roof, render and windows, plus an added garage. Judging by the change of front wall thickness and cracks across the side gable it seems to have an added storey too, but does however retain its seemingly oversized porch, complete with small side windows for visibility up and down the road.

> **West Toll-house, Wisbech**
> (TF 445093)   'T.P.' 'T.B.'
> *Wisbech - Thorney*
>
> About a mile and a half out of town on the north side of the road towards Wisbech St Mary, there was a toll-house guarding the eastern end of the Thorney road.
>
> Just west of the northern end of Cox's Lane, it appeared on the first edition 1" OS map as 'T.P.' and on Greenwood's 1834 map as 'T.B.' The 1842 tithe map shows a roadside building there but without any specific identification.
>
> 'The Gatehouse' almost opposite is most likely a railway building associated with the line that ran parallel to the now diverted north end of Cox's Lane.

Horsey Toll-house, Old Fletton
TL 223960   'Toll'
Private Toll

photo: polystar

Ostensibly modern with its new roof and projecting windows, the core of this building comprises an old toll-house, very similar in form to that at Nene Way, Guyhirn (see p.42). It adjoins the road eastwards from Peterborough towards Whittlesey and March, about a mile to the south of the River Nene.

This road is not recorded as part of any particular turnpike trust's routes and it is thought this building controlled access to a short private road, possibly serving the brick industry. The first edition 1" OS map tends to support this supposition as it is marked with 'Toll' rather than 'T.G.', whilst the 25" map of 1889 shows 'Horsey Toll Gate', with the road to the east marked 'Toll Road'.

Bedford Level Toll-houses
(various locations)
Bedford Level

The Bedford Level north and east of Peterborough contains a number of other instances of 'toll' on the first edition 1" OS map, which may relate to drover's roads.

They include 'Storey's Toll' at TL 231995, 'Toll' at TF 246056 and 250055 north of Causeway Bar (Powder Blue Farm and Buke Horn Toll Farm respectively) and 'Toll' at TL 213923 (Osier Fen). Further north there is also 'Toll Bar' at TF 236079 and 215091 (south and west of Crowland respectively).

Four Lost Peterborough Toll-houses

Lincoln - Peterborough

Peterborough North Toll-houses
(TL 191996 and TL 190999) 'T.P.'
Lincoln Heath - Peterborough

Two toll-houses are indicated very close to each other on the first edition 1" OS map. They are both on the road northwards out of Peterborough towards Lincoln, the southern one shown as 'T.P.', the northern one just 'Toll'.

This may well be a case of a second gate being needed as the city grew out around and engulfed the first, offering too many tempting alternative routes.

Norman Cross Toll-house
(TL 165911) 'T.P.'
Royston - Wansford Bridge

Just north of the village of Stilton at Norman Cross the Royston to Wansford Bridge Trust was enabled in 1751 to add a branch off the Great North Road that ran the six miles or so north-eastwards into Peterborough. This is now the A15 and continues beyond there northwards to Lincoln.

About half a mile along this road there was at one time a toll-house shown as 'T.P.' on the first edition 1" OS map.

Peterborough - Thorney

Newark Toll-house
(TF 204004) 'Toll'
Peterborough - Thorney

Just west of the village of Newark north-east of Peterborough, there was a toll-house about two miles from the centre of the city, controlling the road out to Thorney, which continued from there eastwards to Wisbech.

Shown amongst fields as 'Toll' on the first edition 1" OS map, the toll-house is long gone and the area now thoroughly suburban.

Causeway Toll-house
(TF 248035)
Peterborough - Thorney

About five miles north-east of Peterborough, midway to Thorney, there was a toll-house shown on the first edition 1" OS map as 'Causeway Bar'.

Today nothing remains, but the usage is remembered by the name 'Causeway Toll Farm'.

Elton Toll-house
TL 090938   'T.P.'
Peterborough - Oundle

photo: polystar

The road south-westwards out of Peterborough continued beyond the Great North Road to Oundle in Northamptonshire. Just inside the county boundary there was a toll-house in the village of Elton.

It was on a bend where the road turned southwards to both circumnavigate the grounds of Elton Park and avoid crossing the River Nene twice.

This derelict single storey building, in limestone with a pantile roof, is about the right size and in the right place with good visibility of the road in both directions.

Botolph Bridge Toll-house
(TL 174972)   'T.P.'
Peterborough - Oundle

About two miles south-west of Peterborough there was a toll-house on the road that crossed the Great North Road and continued via Elton to Oundle in Northamptonshire.

More or less opposite the junction with modern day Toll House Road, the outline of a former octagonal ended toll-house can still be seen, its lower wall forming the front garden boundary to no. 439 Oundle Road.

Four More Lost Toll-houses

Royston - Wansford Bridge etc.

Wansford Bridge Toll-house
(TL 076990)   'T.P.'
Royston - Wansford Bridge

Wansford Bridge is where the 'Great North Road' from London via Royston, crossed the River Nene, passing from Huntingdonshire into what was Northamptonshire, which at one time also included Peterborough.

This road was the first turnpike road in the country, originally a 'Justice' trust having been set up in 1663 to repair the road as far as Stilton, renewed in 1710 as far as Wansford Bridge.

Wittering Toll-house
(TF 044036)   'T.P.'
Wansford Bridge - Stamford

North of Wansford Bridge, the Great North Road (now the A1) continues to Stamford in Lincolnshire, passing by the village of Wittering in modern day Cambridgeshire.

Just north of the village, two miles south of Stamford, there was a toll-house, which like the Wansford Bridge site, appeared on the first edition 1" OS map as 'T.P.'

Sawtry Toll-house
(TL 178824)   'Toll Bar'
Royston - Wansford Bridge

A dozen or so miles south of Wansford Bridge, the Great North Road had a further toll-house just south of Sawtry.

The site appears as 'Toll Bar' on the first edition 1" OS map and is at a point where the road forked with a road to the north-west serving the villages of Sawtry and Glatton. 'Toll Bar Cottages' as shown on modern maps is a more recent building.

Ellington Toll-house
(TL 178718)   'T.G.'
Market Harborough - Brampton etc.

About four miles west of Huntingdon there was a toll-house about a mile east of Ellington, controlling access to the eastern end of the road from Brampton towards Market Harborough in Northamptonshire.

A surviving milestone more or less marks the site.

Keyston Toll-house

TL 049762　　　'T.G.'
Market Harborough - Brampton etc.

photo: polystar

The road from Brampton on the Great North Road westwards to Market Harborough in Northamptonshire was turnpiked by a separate trust.

Just west of the village of Bythorn and a mile short of the county boundary, a toll-house was built which has survived since the A604 now by-passes much of the old route.

Quite large, and probably of Victorian date built for toll-farming, it is of two storeys with a classic octagonal bay. Brick built with a slate roof, its character is now somewhat obscured by rendering and plastic windows.

Fayway Toll-house
(TL 067787)　　　'T.G.'
Market Harborough - Brampton etc.

A more northerly heading branch came off this trust's road at Molesworth about a mile east of Bythorn.

The route is interrupted by the now disused airfield north of the village, to the north of which there stood a toll-house on the county border at Fayway.

About two miles further on another 'T.G.' is shown just west of the village of Clopton at TL 057807.

St Ives Bridge Toll-house
TL 313711
Bridge Toll

photo: polystar

Both before the age of turnpikes and after their demise, there was a toll-bridge at St Ives, where the road towards London crossed the River Great Ouse just south of the town. The bridge with its chapel, shown above, dates back to the 15th Century and was built by Ramsey Abbey. Tolls for the use of the bridge were collected at either the doorway or windows that faced onto it and there were also 'Passage Tolls' collected for the use of the river during the forty days of Lent.

After the dissolution of the monasteries the bridge and chapel became Crown property and later in 1628 were sold on to the Earls (later Dukes) of Manchester. The chapel was over the next three centuries variously a private and for some time a public house. By the early 18th Century two additional storeys were added, as shown in the engraving opposite.

The estate was supposed to apply some of the takings to maintain the causeway adjoining, carrying the road over marshy ground to the south. Following the Duke's bankruptcy in 1918, Huntingdonshire County Council took over the bridge and abolished the tolls. They were then given the chapel in 1928, following which the unstable upper floors were removed and the building was restored to some of its former glory.

St Ives Bridge Toll-house
(TL 313711)
Bridge Toll

ST. IVES' BRIDGE.

picture: norris museum

This old engraving shows well the chapel on St Ives Bridge with its two extra storeys, now removed. Also shown in the background is another structure on the bridge, the toll-house built in the 18th Century for collection of the Duke of Manchester's tolls, since the chapel had become a private house.

Possibly octagonal in plan, it sat within one of the bridge's pedestrian refuges and had a conspicuous tall chimney. Use of this toll-house was discontinued in 1822, when the New Bridges toll-house came into use for the Bury to Stratton Turnpike Trust, but it was not removed until the 1920's, serving for a while as a very convenient public urinal.

Oldhurst Toll-house
(approx TL 300770)
Bury - Stratton

The Bury to Stratton turnpike ran from just outside Ramsey, all the way south to Biggleswade in Bedfordshire, passing through St Ives and crossing its bridge en route.

North of St Ives there were two gates, one at Oldhurst and another at Pell's Hole, which was probably where the road today is discontinued for Wyton Airfield. The latter gate was removed to the more strategically placed Green End in 1819.

New Bridges Toll-house & Toll-booth
(TL 312710)
Bury - Stratton

photo: bridget flanagan

The St Ives New Bridges were built in 1822 as a solution to the problem of the lack of repair by the Duke of Manchester of the causeway south of St Ives Bridge. The turnpike trust needed a reliable route and thus paid for the building of the 55 white brick arches of the 'Great White Bridge' and funded it with extra toll charges.

The trust's toll-house at the New Bridges was used for about ten years until its demolition in 1833, by which time they had paid off their debt. The Duke had been obliged to waive his toll at this time, but after 1834 he resumed control and opened the

> **Green End Toll-house, St Ives**
> (TL 312722)   'T.G.'
> *Bury - Stratton*
>
> In 1819 the Bury to Stratton Trust replaced the Pell's Hole gate with a new one at Green End on what was then the north-western edge of St Ives. This location also caught travellers approaching the town from Huntingdon to the west.
>
> Like all of this trust's toll-houses it is now long gone, but like many it did appear on the first edition 1" OS map as 'T.G.'

above toll-booth to catch people in equestrian mode at the northern end of the New Bridges, before they left their horses at the adjoining inns to walk over St Ives Bridge. The booth also collected river tolls, later becoming a road sweeper's store, not being demolished until the 1980's.

Sutton Toll-house (Beds)
(TL 208466)   'T.G.'
Bury - Stratton

photo: bedford record office

This toll-house, the most southerly of the Bury to Stratton Trust's, has at least been recorded in this old photograph. It appears to be of rendered brick construction with a plaintile roof and has side windows for good visibility up and down the road.

Outside our area in Bedfordshire, it is probably typical of the others now lost, such as that at Gamlingay, which was about a mile south of that village, actually on the county boundary between Cambridgeshire and Bedfordshire (TL 234508).

Hemingford Toll-house
(TL 298681)   'T.G.'
Bury - Stratton

About two miles south of the New Bridges, the Bury to Stratton Trust had another toll-house midway between the villages of Hemingford Grey and Hilton, which was also known as Hilton toll-house.

Like all of this trust's toll-houses it is now long gone, but like Sutton and Gamlingay it did appear on the first edition 1" OS map as 'T.G.'

Hartford Toll-house
TL 249722 'T.G.'
Royston - Wansford Bridge

photo: polystar

In 1765 the Royston to Wansford Bridge Trust was enabled to further extend its roads with a branch from Huntingdon north-eastwards to Somersham, thereby connecting through via Chatteris to the Wisbech road.

Just outside Huntingdon, on the south-west of Hartford village this toll-house was built, typically very close to the road edge.

Nowadays known as Toll Bar Cottage, it has been extensively modernised with new windows, a render finish and the porch blocked in: only its position really gives a clue to its former use.

Waresley Toll-house
(TL 240539) 'T.G.'
Bury - Stratton

About a mile north of Gamlingay there was a further toll-house at Waresley, south west of the village of that name and adjoining an entrance to Waresley Park. It was on the old county boundary between Huntingdonshire and Cambridgeshire.

Further north at Eltisley, another appearance of 'T.G.' on the first edition 1" OS map looks like it should be on this road, but is actually for a toll-house belonging to the St Neots to Cambridge Trust (see p.60).

Godmanchester Toll-house
TL 244711　　　'T.G.'
Royston - Wansford Bridge

photo: polystar

All traffic between Huntingdon and the south had to cross Huntingdon Bridge. Consequently a toll-house was built on the Great North Road at Godmanchester, on the causeway approaching the Bridge from the south, where the road ran very close to the River Great Ouse and there was no alternative route.

Fortunately the road here is now by-passed and the building survives by virtue of its grade II listing. Of two storeys, in white brick with a tiled mansard roof it has a small bay very close to the road edge and two side windows in the southern gable end ideal for keeping an eye on approaching traffic.

Caxton Toll-house
(TL 299599)　　　'T.G.'
Royston - Wansford Bridge

About seven very straight miles south of Godmanchester there was a further toll-house on the Great North Road (originally the Roman road Ermine Street).

It was about half a mile south of the Caxton Gibbet, where the Cambridge to St Neots road crosses and a mile north of the village of Caxton itself. It appeared on the first edition 1" OS map as 'T.G.'

Four Lost Toll-houses near St Neots

Great Staughton - Wellingborough

Kimbolton Toll-house
(TL 096680)   'T.G.'
Great Staughton - Wellingborough

The road west from St Neots went to Wellingborough in Northamptonshire by way of Great Staughton and Kimbolton before it left the former county of Huntingdonshire.

The 1847 Kimbolton tithe map shows at the west end of the village both the building on the north side of the road and a bar across it, but without further detail.

Stoneley Toll-house
(TL 116663)   'T.G.'
Great Staughton - Wellingborough

About two miles south-east of Kimbolton there was another toll-house on the Wellingborough road at Stoneley.

All three of the toll-houses in this area are shown on the first edition 1" OS map as 'T.G.'

Great Staughton Toll-house
(TL 126647)   'T.G.'
Great Staughton - Lavendon

A more southerly branch off the Great Staughton to Wellingborough road, heading towards Lavendon in Buckinghamshire, was authorised by an act in 1802.

A toll-house controlling access to this route, which crossed all of Bedfordshire, was built at Great Staughton itself about a quarter mile off the Wellingborough road.

Little Paxton Toll-house
(TL 186635)   'T.G.'
Biggleswade - Alconbury

Something of a competitor with the Great North Road can be found in the route northwards from London via Baldock, Biggleswade and St Neots, that is now the A1.

The two routes combined at Alconbury Hill, north-west of Huntingdon, the western alternative being controlled by the Biggleswade to Alconbury trust, which had a toll-house at Little Paxton, just north of St Neots.

Wintringham Toll-house
TL 219599   'T.G.'
St Neots - Cambridge

photo: polystar

About two miles east of St Neots, the first toll-house on this trust's route towards Cambridge was at Wintringham. The building survives opposite the entrance way to Wintringham Hall, albeit very close to the busy modern road.

It is an otherwise nondescript brick built bungalow with a pyramidal hipped tiled roof and modern metal windows. However its distinctive projecting porch, even closer to the road with two small side windows, gives away its former use.

Eynesbury Toll-house
(TL 272599)   'T.G.'
Potton - St Neots

The turnpike trust for this route, now the B1046, connecting across between the Bury to Stratton road and the Biggleswade to Alconbury road came quite late in 1814.

There was a toll-house just south-east of Eynesbury, now on the outskirts of St Neots, which was shown as 'T.G.' on the first edition 1" OS map.

Four Lost Toll-houses west of Cambridge

St Neots - Cambridge

Cambridge - Arrington Br

Eltisley Toll-house
(TL 272599)   'T.G.' 'T.B.'
St Neots - Cambridge

At the north end of the village of Eltisley, where the St Neots to Cambridge road crosses the Bury to Stratton road, the former trust had a toll-house, controlling the road eastwards to Cambridge.

The 1841 tithe map clearly shows the building and toll-bar guarding the way and a revised tithe apportionment of 1888 lists the triangular plot in the fork as 'Toll Gate Piece', although the building had by then gone.

Grantchester Toll-house
(TL 421568)   'T.G.' 'T.B.'
Cambridge - Arrington Bridge

The road towards Potton and Biggleswade in Bedfordshire, south-west out of Cambridge was guarded by a toll-house about a mile north-west of Grantchester. The first part of this road was controlled by the Cambridge to Arrington Bridge trust.

The site of the toll-house is now under a roundabout, part of junction 12 of the M11.

Coton Toll-house
(TL 413594)   'T.G.'
St Neots - Cambridge

The western approach of this turnpike trust's road into Cambridge was guarded by a toll-house just north of the village of Coton. Here roads came off the main road south to Coton itself and north-west to Madingley. Nothing remains at this site, but it was shown on the first edition 1" OS map as 'T.G.'

About four miles further west on the main road, modern maps show 'Childerley Gate' at TL 355598. This may have turnpike connections.

Wimpole Lodge Toll-house
(TL 489173)   'T.G.'
Cambridge - Arrington Bridge

The further end of this first section of road towards Bedfordshire was controlled by a toll-house at Wimpole Lodge. It was about half a mile before the end of this trust's road at Arrington Bridge, which carried the Great North Road over the River Cam.

Beyond here the road passed into the hands of the Arrington Bridge to Potton trust.

Croydon Toll-house
TL 314484
Arrington Bridge - Potton

photo: polystar

About two miles west of the Arrington toll-house there was another at Lower Road, Croydon, which fortunately survives.

Also described in the RCHM(E) 'Inventory', it was 'single storeyed, of white brick with slated roofs; c.1826'. Unfortunately like so many fine gault brick buildings it has now been rendered over and painted.

This route continued the Cambridge to Arrington Bridge Trust's road south-westwards out of Cambridge. About four miles further on, over the border into Bedfordshire, there was another toll-house at Wrestlingworth (TL 260469), shown as 'T.G.' on the first edition 1" OS map.

Arrington Toll-house
(TL 332489)   'T.G.' 'T.B.'
Arrington Bridge - Potton

Guarding the entrance to what is now the B1042 Potton road to the west off the Great North Road, there was a toll-house at Arrington.

Described in RCHM(E)'s 'Inventory of Historical Monuments in the County of Cambridge' (1968) as 'one storey, gault brick and slated roof; c.1825', it has since been demolished for a roundabout. It was on the north-west corner of the junction and is shown on the 1837 Arrington tithe map marked as 'Toll House'.

Four Lost Royston Toll-houses

Tring - Bourn Bridge

Litlington Toll-house
(TL 329401)   'Toll Bar'
Tring - Bourn Bridge

On the county border, nothing is shown for this toll-house on the Litlington tithe map, which suggests it was actually on the south side of the road in Hertfordshire.

This long distance road from that county followed the line of the 'Icknield Way' Roman road for many miles passing through both Baldock and Royston.

Whittlesford Toll-house
(TL 488472)   'T.G.'
Tring - Bourn Bridge

East of Royston the road diverges northwards away from the Icknield Way to its end at Bourn Bridge over the River Granta near Abington.

About three miles before this it crosses the River Cam at Whittlesford Station, north of Duxford. Here there was a toll-house adjoining the river crossing and sensibly half a mile west of the junction of this road with the Chesterford to Cambridge route that follows the east bank of the river.

Cambridge - Royston etc.

Royston Toll-house (Herts)
(TL 359407)
Cambridge - Royston etc.

Situated in the centre of Royston, this toll-house was sited at what was a busy cross-roads that has now become a roundabout.

The Melbourn tithe map of 1839 shows a small plot on the north-eastern corner of the cross-roads, described in the apportionment as 'Tollhouse & Yard' owned by 'Trustees of the Hauxton & Dunsbridge Turnpike Road'.

Melbourn Toll-house
(TL 370433)   'Toll Bar'
Cambridge - Royston etc.

A mile south-west of Melbourn and about two miles north-east of the Royston site, there was another toll-house operated by this trust.

Possibly either an earlier or later site, it was shown as 'Toll bar' on the first edition 1" OS map, but seems absent from the tithe records.

Trumpington Toll-house
TL 446547
Chesterford - Newmarket / Cambridge

photo: polystar

In 1724 the road from Chesterford, south-east of Cambridge, was the earliest route into the city to be turnpiked, followed in 1725 by the route from Fowlmere more to the south. This toll-house stands where the two routes met, about three miles south of Cambridge, in what is now the suburb of Trumpington. It would have controlled both these routes and the later one approaching the city from Royston.

Grade II listed, in the local white gault brick with a slate roof, it is a classic octagonal ended early 19th Century toll-house with a doorway facing the road and a blanked out window above where the toll-board would have been placed.

Hauxton Toll-house
(TL 432528)   'T.G.'
Trumpington - Fowlmere

About two miles south of Trumpington, there was a further toll-house just north of the village of Hauxton.

Situated where the road crossed the River Cam, it would have controlled traffic from both Fowlmere and the route slightly further west from Royston, now the A10.

Great Chesterford Toll-house (Essex)
TL 505428
Essex & Herts

photo: polystar

In the far north-western corner of Essex, near the Cambridgeshire border at Stump Cross, this building known as 'Mill Cottage', very much looks like a toll-house with its roadside entrance porch.

Timber-framed and plastered it is grade II listed and the description reads 'said to have been The Old Toll House'. Its good position commanding views on a junction would seem to corroborate this.

The only slight problem is that the early first edition 1" OS map shows a 'T.P.' about half a mile further south, in Little Chesterford at TL 510421, where a more modern house stands today.

Stapleford Toll-house
(TL 469518)   'T.G.'
Chesterford - Newmarket / Cambridge

The continuation of the Essex and Herts Trust road north of Great Chesterford was under the control of the Chesterford to Newmarket Heath and Cambridge Trust. Accordingly it forks at Stump Cross on the Cambridgeshire border.

The Cambridge branch of this trust's roads had a toll-house at Stapleford, roughly midway from Stump Cross, and about three miles before the road reached Trumpington south of the city.

Paper Mill Toll-house
TL 473595 'T.G.'
Godmanchester - Newmarket Heath

photo: polystar

The Godmanchester to Newmarket turnpike came right through Cambridge on its way eastwards, becoming the modern A1303 east of the city.

On the way out of Cambridge, understandably in Newmarket Road, stands the grade II listed Paper Mill toll-house, built of local white gault clay bricks with a slate roof.

It is single storey with a large octagonal ended bay containing a doorway facing the road, and is now known as The Round House.

Newmarket Heath Toll-house
(TL 619614)   'T.G.' 'T.B.'
Chesterford - Newmarket / Cambridge

About two miles out of Newmarket, roughly on the border with Cambridgeshire where the road crosses 'Devil's Ditch', there once stood a toll-house controlling the south-western approaches to the town. Here the road forked, the south-western leg forming the eastern part of the Chesterford to Cambridge and Newmarket turnpike.

The toll-house is shown on the 1842 Burwell tithe map, listed in the apportionment as 'Turnpike House & Garden' owned by 'Trustees of Turnpike Road'.

Four Lost Toll-houses around Cambridge

Godmanchester - Newmarket Heath etc.

Fenstanton Toll-house
(TL 312685)   'T.G.'
Godmanchester - Newmarket Heath

About four miles east of Godmanchester along what was an old Roman route from Huntingdon to Cambridge, the first toll-house was at Fenstanton, shown on the first edition 1" OS map as 'T.G.'

Nearer Cambridge, but about a mile off the main road the same map shows a 'Toll Bar' just south of the village of Longstanton (TL 389656). Nowadays known as Bar Farm, it is unclear whether this was a turnpike route, the minor road north here leading through Willingham on to Haddenham and then Chatteris.

Chesterton Road Toll-house
(TL 447592)   'T.G.'
Cambridge - Ely etc.

The first part of the turnpike route out of Cambridge northwards to Ely ran through Chesterton and Milton, roughly parallel to and about a mile east of an old Roman road.

Access to this route was controlled by a toll-house in Chesterton Road, north of the city, shown on the first edition 1" OS map as 'T.G.'

Huntingdon Road Toll-house
(TL 442594)   'T.G.'
Godmanchester - Newmarket Heath

On the approach to Cambridge from the north-west, there was also a toll-house in Huntingdon Road, roughly where two roads joined from the north.

One of these is now the B1049 to Histon and Cottenham, the other a now lost Roman road, which further out forms part of the Cambridge to Ely road (A10).

Red Cross Toll-house
(TL 470551)   'T.G.' 'T.B.'
Haverhill - Shelford

Just out of Cambridge to the south-east, the first edition 1" OS map indicates a toll-gate at Red Cross, north of Great Shelford.

This site is now on the southern edge of the city very near Addenbrooke's Hospital, the toll-house probably lost for road improvements.

Abington Toll-house
TL 533488
Haverhill - Shelford

photo: polystar

Known as 'Toll Gate Cottage' and grade II listed, this toll-house is shown on an old photograph with a doorway between the two windows facing onto Linton Road, which here follows the south bank of the River Granta. The building is timber-framed and rendered with a thatched roof, unusual in toll-houses.

Curiously 'T.G.' is shown on the first edition 1" OS map in two places half a mile either side of this location. One is at Little Abington (TL 534494), the other at Great Abington (TL 531481), but no trace remains of anything at these locations.

Horseheath Toll-house
(TL 633469)   'T.G.'
Haverhill - Shelford

At the far end of this turnpike trust's route, almost into Suffolk, there was a toll-house at Horseheath about three miles before Haverhill.

Now long gone, it was shown on the first edition 1" OS map as 'T.G.', as was another toll-house nearby at Withersfield (TL 653477). The tithe map apportionment of 1840 listed the latter as 'Turnpike House & Garden', owned by 'Trustees of Turnpike Road'.

Burwell Toll-house
(TL 608695) 'Toll Bar'
Private Toll

photo: cambridge antiquarian society

This old photograph shows the toll-gate on Ness Road at Burwell, with what was probably the toll-house adjoining, brick built with a slate roof and big side windows facing up the road towards Fordham.

Although well documented at its closure in December 1905, this is rather late for a turnpike trust, so it remains unclear who controlled this minor route. The site is commemorated by a memorial stone (see p.28) and shown as 'Toll Bar' on the first edition 1" OS map.

Snailwell Toll-house
(TL 655648) 'T.G.' 'T.B.'
Bury St Edmunds - Newmarket

The toll-house at Snailwell, about a mile north-east of Newmarket, controlled this approach to the town and was built right on the county boundary with Suffolk. Known as Moulton Gate, it was at a fork on the north-western side of the road.

The Bury St Edmunds road to the east follows the county boundary for some miles towards another toll-gate at Kentford (TL 709668). The Thetford road to the north-east was under the control of the Thetford to Newmarket Trust and after some four miles across Cambridgeshire there was another toll-house at Red Lodge, just inside the Suffolk border, and just inside the parish of Freckenham (TL 693698).

5.0 Appendix: The Impostors

Buildings in Cambridgeshire that are not Toll-houses

When researching and looking for toll-houses in any county, one's first attempts will undoubtedly focus on various octagonal ended buildings near the roadside that seem to offer themselves up as likely candidates.

We have seen from the foregoing gazetteer that in Cambridgeshire this type of toll-house, as found at Trumpington or Chatteris, is certainly not the norm. In fact the norm for the area appears to be the foursquare two storey house or single storey bungalow, sometimes with a central porch and the requisite side gable windows for vision up and down the road, such as those found at Littleport, Godmanchester, Croydon or Wintringham.

In order to prevent the inevitable "but what about the toll-house at ....?" type questions that might follow the publication of this book, the following appendix includes a fair selection of octagonal ended buildings from around the county. It seems that many such buildings were built, mainly as lodges or cottages ornées. Thus the octagonal form is certainly not unknown in Cambridgeshire as the following pages will testify, it is just that the toll-house builders chose not to use it for some reason.

These 'impostors' are presented in roughly the same order as the main gazetteer of toll-houses, i.e. from the Isle of Ely west across the county to Huntingdonshire, then south and east back to Cambridge itself. Many of these are from parishes where a toll-house was expected to be found, and many of them have for varying lengths of time led the author slightly astray. It is hoped that diligent research has by now weeded out all such impostors from the gazetteer proper, so that they are all relegated to this appendix..

The author will of course be pleased to hear enquiries of the form "but what about the impostor at ....?", they almost warrant a book of their own!

Round House, Mepal
TL 441808

Although this octagonal building with 'gothick' windows adjoins a former turnpike road, it is not a toll-house.

The main road now by-passes the village of Mepal and the building survives, described in its grade II listing as a lodge, although there is no drive and it is unclear where the main house might have been.

Built fairly close to the road in white brick with a modern plaintile roof, the octagonal plan is set with a vertex nearest the road and its porch is off to one side.

photo: polystar

Round House, Doddington
TL 404909

This small octagonal cottage at the north end of the village of Doddington, north of Chatteris, sits with its doorway facing the road. Again this was a former turnpike road, between Chatteris and March, but the building is not a toll-house.

Like the Mepal example it is grade II listed, but this time described as just a cottage. Very much in the cottage ornée tradition it is built of rendered brick and has 'gothick' windows and a thatched roof.

photo: polystar

House, Huntingdon
TL 235717

This octagonal ended building with good all round visibility was at one time on the outskirts of Huntingdon.

Situated in George Street, on the west side of the town, it was a semi-detached house, part of a development called Sandwich Villas.

Built in white brick with a slate roof, the walls are now painted white and it is used as a dentist's surgery.

The adjoining property exhibits the original materials, but does not have the rather oversized bay.

photo: polystar

Sheep Market Toll-house, St Ives
TL 316712

This rather ornate Victorian building in white brick with stone dressings at Sheep Market, St Ives is listed grade II and described by English Heritage as 'formerly a Toll House'.

Although the Chatteris Ferry to Somersham Turnpike Trust's roads were extended to Sheep Market, the town centre position makes it more likely this building was for market use, as gates here would be of little use for controlling access to a road.

Interestingly the Duke of Manchester was the recipient of market tolls in St Ives and may well have had this built before he went bankrupt.

photo: polystar

Lodge, Wimpole
TL 321526

This octagonal cottage adjoins the main Royston to Wansford Bridge road about two miles north of Arrington, where its distinctive slate roof and octagonal white brick chimney are clearly visible above the roadside hedge.

Doubtless built during the turnpike era, it is not however a toll-house but a grade II listed lodge to nearby Wimpole Hall. Probably originally in white brick, the walls are now rendered and it now has had a modern extension added to the south.

photo: polystar

Lodge, Newton
TL 436493

Grade II listed and described by English Heritage as a 'Toll-house, now lodge house', the latter is certainly true as it is sited adjoining the entrance to Newton Manor, which it guards well.

As for 'toll-house', apart from its design there is no evidence, as it is not on a former turnpike road, indeed the road here is but a minor rural cul-de-sac. Its construction in white gault brick also means it is unlikely to have been moved as a timber-framed building might be.

photo: polystar

Conservator's House, Horningsea
TL 502644

The Conservators of the River Cam controlled the river from Bottisham Lock upstream towards the city of Cambridge.

Their headquarters building at Horningsea, shown here, is a grade II listed building dated 1842, about fifty years ahead of the fashion for dutch gables. It is built in the local white gault brick and has plaintiles on its roof made of the same light coloured material.

Although described as a toll-house, whilst tolls were probably collected here, it was not the building's main purpose.

photo: polystar

Jesus Lock Cottage, Cambridge
TL 450592

This fine white gault brick building with its slate roof and octagonal bay looks the way a toll-house is often imagined, expressing in its shape and forward projection that it involved an element of control in its use.

It does not however front onto a road but adjoins Jesus Lock in central Cambridge where the waters and traffic of the River Cam are controlled by a lock under the auspices of the 'Conservators of the River Cam'.

photo: polystar

Coldham's Gatehouse, Cambridge
TL 470587

This small gatehouse adjoining Coldham's Common to the east of Cambridge centre has the look of a toll-house about it, was built at about the right time and did indeed perform a similar function.

It was in fact a gatehouse controlling access to and from the common, and was used for the weighing of coprolites mined there.

It is built in the local gault clay white brick with a slate roof and has three prominent chimneys and a window at the end for keeping an eye on traffic.

photo: polystar

6.0 Bibliography

Albert, W. 1972 *Turnpike Road System in England 1663-1840* Cambridge

Alderton, D. & Booker, J. 1980 *The Industrial Archaeology of East Anglia* Batsford

Burn-Murdoch, B. 2001 *St Ives Bridge and Chapel* Norris Museum

Chatwin, C.P. 1961 *East Anglia and Adjoining Areas* British Regional Geology HMSO

Clifford, S. & King, A. (eds) 1993 *Local Distinctiveness* Common Ground

Cossons, A. 1951 *The Turnpike Roads of Norfolk* Norfolk and Norwich Archaeological Society vol.XXX part III

Cruickshank, D. & Wyld, P. 1975 *London: The Art of Georgian Building* Architectural Press

Flanagan, B. 2005 *The New Bridges* Flanagan

Freethy, R. 1987 *Turnpikes and Toll Houses of Lancashire* Countryside

Haines, C. 2000 *Marking The Miles A History of English Milestones* Haines

Harris, R. (ed) (no date) *Weald & Downland Open Air Museum Guidebook*

Haynes, R. & Slocombe, I. 2004 *Wiltshire Toll Houses* Hobnob Press

Mogg, E. 1829 *Paterson's Roads* London

Mowl, T. & Earnshaw, B. 1985 *Trumpet at a Distant Gate* Waterstone

Pawson, E. 1977 *Transport and Economy: The Turnpike Roads of Eighteenth Century Britain* Academic Press

Searle, M. 1930 *Turnpikes and Toll-Bars* Hutchinson

Serjeant, W.R. & Penrose, D.G. (eds) 1973 *Suffolk Turnpikes* E Suffolk RO

Smith, P. 1970 *The Turnpike Age* Luton Museum and Art Gallery

Wright, G.N. 1992 *Turnpike Roads* Shire

Of Related Interest:

Federation of Old Cornwall Societies:
The Toll-houses of Cornwall
Patrick Taylor   2001   £7.95
ISBN 0 902660 29 2   80pp

Companion volume to the present one, contains a similar introductory essay and history of the turnpike roads in Cornwall, followed by an extensive gazetteer of toll-houses and their former sites.

"A useful detailed county study with photographs of high quality" *Industrial Archaeology Review*

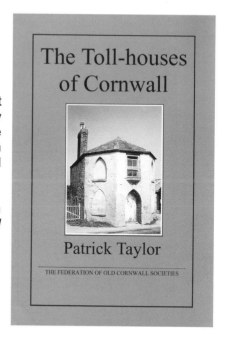

Polystar Press:

Books by Patrick Taylor:

The Toll-houses of Suffolk
ISBN 978 1 907154 00 3   2009

The Toll-houses of Norfolk
ISBN 978 1 907154 02 7   2009

The Toll-houses of Essex
ISBN 978 1 907154 04 1   2010

Books by Tim Jenkinson
          & Patrick Taylor:

The Toll-houses of South Devon
ISBN 978 1 907154 01 0   2009

The Toll-houses of North Devon
ISBN 978 1 907154 03 4   2010

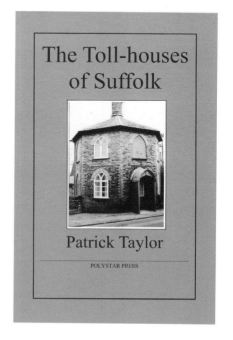